**COURANT
COMPUTER SCIENCE
SYMPOSIUM 4**
MARCH 1 - 2, 1971

ALGORITHM SPECIFICATION

Edited by **RANDALL RUSTIN**
Courant Institute of Mathematical Sciences
New York University

PRENTICE-HALL, INC., Englewood Cliffs, New Jersey

Library of Congress Cataloging in Publication Data
Main entry under title

Algorithm specification.

    (Courant computer science symposium, 4, Mar. 1-2, 1971)
    1. Electronic digital computers—Programming—Congresses. 2. Programming languages (Electronic computers)—Congresses. 3. Algorithms—Congresses.
I. Rustin, Randall, ed. II. Title III. Series.
QA76.6.A4   001.6.42   72-512
ISBN 0-13-022319-0

© 1972
by Prentice-Hall, Inc., Englewood Cliffs, N.J.

All rights reserved. No part of this book may be reproduced in any form or by any means without permission in writing from the publisher.

10 9 8 7 6 5 4 3 2 1

Printed in United States of America

PRENTICE-HALL INTERNATIONAL, INC., London
PRENTICE-HALL OF AUSTRALIA, PTY. LTD., Sydney
PRENTICE-HALL OF CANADA, LTD., Toronto
PRENTICE-HALL OF INDIA PRIVATE LIMITED, New Delhi
PRENTICE-HALL OF JAPAN, INC., Tokyo

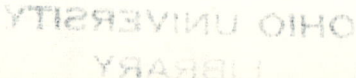

ALGORITHM
SPECIFICATION

**Prentice-Hall
Series in Automatic Computation**
George Forsythe, editor

CONTENTS

Foreword
Introduction
List of Participants

Jacob T. Schwartz   1
Principles of Specification Language Design with Some Observations Concerning the Utility of Specification Languages

Malcolm C. Harrison   39
Declarative and Extendable Languages

Glenn Manacher   61
Low Level Data Structure Handling in a High Level Language

H. R. Strong   81
Flowchartable Recursive Specification

John Bruno and Kenneth Steiglitz   97
The Expression of Algorithms by Charts

T. Lyons and John Bruno   117
An Interactive System for Program Verification

FOREWORD

The series of books of which the present volume is the fourth originated in a symposium series in areas of current interest in computer science which were presented by the Computer Science Department of the Courant Institute of Mathematical Sciences of New York University. The participants were drawn from the academic and industrial communities to allow the interchange of ideas between these two groups. They were selected for their knowledge of and active involvement in the fields to be discussed.

The emphasis at the meeting was on the discussion of open problems rather than on the presentation of solved problems. References for greater detail have been appended to the papers.

Written versions of the talks were not submitted prior to the meeting. Speakers had the option of editing their transcripts or providing written equivalents. It should be clear which papers are most faithful to the spoken word. The atmosphere of the meetings was intended to be informal, and discussion was encouraged by allocating time for question periods and breaks after each talk.

Support for the meetings was provided by a grant from the Mathematics Program of the Office of Naval Research. I would like to thank Dr. Leila Bram, Director of the Mathematics Program, for her interest in and involvement with the symposia; and Professor Jacob T. Schwartz, Chairman of the NYU Computer Science Department, for the general conception of the series and the choice of specific topics.

I would also like to express my gratitude to Ms Linda Adamson, without whose typing and editing assistance these volumes would not exist; and to Ms Connie Engle, without whose administrative and organizational help I fear the symposia would not have existed.

        Randall Rustin
        Administrator of the Symposia

INTRODUCTION

The papers in this volume deal with attempts to specify algorithms so that they are acceptable to man and machine.

When specifying an algorithm without the necessity for actual computation, natural language or the language of mathematics is often satisfactory. The former provides intuitive grasp, the latter precision. However, neither is sufficient in specifying an algorithm for which computations, particularly automatic, are to be carried out. Natural language lacks succinctness, ambiguity is likely, precision is difficult, and as yet, no computer is able to understand it. Mathematical notation, although it is precise, usually leaves the sequence of processing implicit. Ideally then, one would like to express an algorithm with the intuitiveness of natural language, but with the precision of mathematics.

In his talk on principles of specification languages, Jacob T. Schwartz presents a brief description of his set-language, SETL, which has been designed to rigorously specify abstract algorithms in a form that is also acceptable as a programming language. Advantages of such a language include the ability to maintain the distinction between the abstract and the concrete as long as possible in order to examine intrinsic properties of an algorithm or a class of algorithms. Essentially, we would like to be able to evaluate the objects of interest without the trappings of data structure and representation constraints. (An algorithm is spoken of as *abstract* when the arrangement of the data is left unspecified; the assumption being that there is some quintessential aspect of the algorithm that can be described independent of the data structuring. When, in addition, some arrangement of the data, the mode of data access and the operations on the data are specified, we speak of the algorithm as *concrete*.)

In part today's profusion of programming languages is a result of the desire to felicitously express specific actions on sets of specific data types. The availability of a programming language in which a class of algorithms is easily expressible tends to reinforce activity leading to greater development of that class of algorithms. However, this availability has the obvious consequence that an algorithm easily expressible in one language may be expressed only with great difficulty, if at all, in another. This has led to the intense development of "general purpose" programming languages; i.e., languages powerful enough to express algorithms for a wide variety of data types, thus broadening the class of algorithms surveyable in a single context.

When language operators relate data types simple enough to be accessed by internal machine actions, it is possible to construct reasonably efficient translators. However, for more complex data types the correspondence between the language description of the type and its internal mapping is quite complicated and basically out of the control of the language user. Machine coding, of course, provides maximal control, but the set of operations provided by the set of available machines is too primitive for the natural conceptualization of problems and furthermore is in no way unique from machine to machine. Thus, this is not seriously considered an alternative mode of algorithm specification. Glenn Manacher's ESPL is a low-level, high-level-like language that, with a minimum of machine dependence, provides the programmer with the capability of greater control (and corresponding machine efficiency) of the internal representation of the program. The class of data structures available is enlarged because the data structures do not have to be as stereotyped as in the usual high-level languages.

An alternative to a general purpose language for the specification of algorithms is to allow a mechanism for the extension of a programming language. The core language has to be chosen in such a way that it is reasonably easy for the programmer to extend the language. Malcolm Harrison discusses this aspect of language design in terms of BALM, an extendable language which he designed and implemented.

Other efforts have been to reduce a class of algorithms to those of another class for which a reasonably acceptable form of expression already exists. This might be looked at as a reduction to some canonical form. Perhaps the simplest and most "canonical" form for expressing algorithms is that of the flowchart. The assumption being that from this form, implementation into any one of a number of programming languages is straightforward. There is value then in attempting to enlarge the class of functions which are flowchartable. H.R. Strong's paper is a tutorial on the specification of those recursive forms that are flowchartable.

John Bruno and Kenneth Steiglitz also begin with algorithms in the form of flowcharts. However, here a characterization of a subset of the class of flowcharts, namely those without *go-to*'s, is defined in order to give an alternative method for the redefinition of an algorithm, and the formal definition of flowcharts and D-charts. Lyons and Bruno describe an "interactive system based on a *go-to*-less, D-chart type of programming language".

This volume in no way purports to be definitive in its representation of past or present activities. It is, however, hoped that it represents an interesting sampling of some of the more recent active research in the area.

Randall Rustin

PARTICIPANTS

Ames, Gail	IBM Corporation
Angell, Mary	IBM Corporation, Yorktown
Bob, Murray	Brooklyn College
Bober, Raymond R.	Stevens Inst. of Technology
Chang, Shi-Kuo	Cornell University
Charmonman, Sak	University of Missouri
Chen, Stephen	Bell Telephone Labs.
Doody, James V., Jr.	Information Resources, Inc.
Fisher, Gerald, Jr.	Illinois Inst. of Technology
Flanagan, Joe	IBM Corporation, SRI
Fox, David	Leasco Data Processing Equip.
Frazer, W.D.	IBM Corporation
Frommer, S.	New York University
Gerhart, Susan	Carnegie-Mellon University
Goldstein, Max	New York University
Goodenough, John B.	U.S. Air Force Electronic Sys.
Haggerty, Joseph P.	Bell Telephone Labs.
Hammer, Michael M.	M.I.T.
Harris, Arthur D.S.	Brookhaven National Lab.
Homer, Eugene	Long Island University
Howden, William	Univ. of California, Irvine
Johnson, Beverly	Barnard, Columbia
Joshi, Aravind K.	University of Pennsylvania
Kahane, Joseph	Queens College
Levy, Leon S.	University of Delaware
Loveman, David B.	Air Force Inst. of Technology
Mazur, John	Information Resources, Inc.
Ostrinsky, Renah	Brooklyn College
Pessin, Arthur L.	Rider College & Rutgers Univ.
Raver, Norman	IBM Corporation, ASDD
Sherman, Ron	IBM Corporation
Smith, David	Columbia University
Sondak, Norman E.	Worcester Polytechnic Inst.
Tsao, John H.	IBM Corporation
Urion, Henry K.	Dartmouth College
Walker, Sue A.	IBM Corporation, Yorktown

PRINCIPLES OF SPECIFICATION LANGUAGE DESIGN WITH SOME OBSERVATIONS CONCERNING THE UTILITY OF SPECIFICATION LANGUAGES

Jacob T. Schwartz
Courant Institute of Mathematical Sciences
New York University

The general outlines of a new programming language, designated SETL, whose dictions are drawn from the mathematical theory of sets, will be presented. Examples of the use of this language as an algorithm specification tool will be given. Some general comments on the nature of programming languages will also be made.

The work that is the subject of this paper has its roots in certain musings concerning the relationship between mathematics and programming in which the author has from time to time indulged. On the one hand, programming is concerned with the specification of algorithmic processes in a form ultimately machinable. On the other, mathematics describes some of these same processes, or in some cases merely their results, almost always in a much more succinct form, yet in a form whose precision all will admit. Comparing the two, one gets a very strong even if initially confused impression that programming is somehow more difficult than it should be. Why is this? That is, why must there be so large a gap between a logically precise specification of an object to be constructed and a programming language account of a method for its construction? Part of the answer may be given in a single word: efficiency. However, as we shall see, we will want to take this word in a rather different sense than that which ordinarily preoccupies programmers.

More specifically, the implicit dictions used in the language of mathematics, which dictions give this language much of its power, often imply searches over infinite or at any rate very large sets. Programming algorithms realizing these same constructions must of necessity be equivalent procedures devised so as to cut down on the ranges that will be searched to find the objects one is looking for. In this sense, one may say that programming is optimization and that mathematics is what programming becomes when we forget optimization and program in the manner appropriate for an infinitely fast machine with infinite amounts of memory. At the most fundamental level, it is the mass of optimizations with which it is burdened that makes programming so cumbersome a process, and one must always remember that the sluggishness of this process is the principal obstacle to the development of the computer art.

These reflections suggest that some of the weight of programming be thrown off by passing from the programming dictions ordinarily used to a more highly "mathematicized" language. Our hope to be able to make something of this general idea is raised by the observation that efficiency has two rather different sides. One is mathematical and abstract in character. What intermediate logical constructs must be built as a process proceeds, and how large are the sets of logical objects over which searches must be extended during such a process? The other side of efficiency is machine-related and basically twofold. First we must ask the question of inner loop efficiency: Into what tabular representations can necessary abstract structures be mapped with advantage, and once this representation is established, how efficiently can the necessary coded processes be made to effect these tables? Then we must ask a fundamental question related ultimately to the speed chasm which separates electronic from electro-mechanical memories: How large are the data sets with which an algorithm will force us to deal? How can these data sets best be staged between different grades of memory so as to hurry the completion of an algorithmic process? We may remark that machine-related efficiency issues are apt to have as much or more to do with these memory management problems as with problems of inner loop coding, even though most programmers, especially those with an assembly-language background and bias, tend to think more of the latter. Our hypothetical mathematicized programming language would practically by definition mask all machine-related efficiency issues almost completely. There is, however, no reason why it should hide these more abstract issues of process design which can easily have a more important bearing on efficiency. Indeed — and this is one of the benefits for which we may hope — it should, by masking the former, enhance our ability to concentrate on the latter.

The foregoing considerations lead one to suspect that a programming language modeled after an appropriate version of the formal language of mathematics might allow a programming style with some of the succinctness of mathematics and that this might ultimately enable us to express and to experiment with more complex algorithms than are now within reach. The notion of language that appears here then demands additional clarification. Speaking very generally, a computer language is a set of notations referencing objects and processes, and satisfying all the following constraints:

    1. A formal distinction between well-formed and ill-formed programs exists, and a "syntax checker" capable of administering this distinction can be built.

    2. That class of objects and processes to which well-formed programs refer can be defined rigorously.

3. A "compiler" capable of transforming a
well-formed program into the objects and processes
that it represents can be built. These objects can
in fact be represented within a computer, and the
processes can in fact be carried out.

Since it refers as a matter of course to
infinite sets, the language of mathematics has only
the first two of these properties, not the third.
Nevertheless, it is clear that in searching for a
mathematicized programming language we will wish to
start from some appropriate version of the language
of mathematics. With which of the several variants
of formal mathematics that might be contenders
shall we begin? It is not unreasonable to begin
with set theory, formally represented, let us say,
in its von Neumann-Bernays form. This is a language
relatively free of artifice, close to the heuristic
spirit of informal mathematics, and a formal system
with one or another version of which there is a
great body of satisfactory experience. In particular, we know that using the very small and simple
set of primitives that this language embodies that
the whole structure of mathematics, from abstract
algebra to complex function theory, can be built up
rapidly, intuitively, and in a manner largely free
of irritating artificialities. Taking this as our
starting point, our problem becomes the following:
Adapt set-theory to be machinable.

Unless one feels more confidence than at present
seems justifiable in one's ability to cope with the
still largely impenetrable difficulties of mechanical
theorem proving, one will have to calculate not with
logical formula's but with sets actually enumerated,
and this means that one must think in terms of a
language that will be capable of dealing only with
finite sets. Given that this is our plan, we must
first inquire as to the extent to which the primitive
notions embodied in the axioms of set theory are
consistent with such a restriction. An easy examination shows that -- with the single and obvious
exception of the axiom of infinity, which asserts
that there exists a set consisting of all the
integers -- every other basic construction of set

theory leads naturally from finite sets only to
finite sets. Thus to begin designing a language
we have only to abandon the mathematician's habit
of referring to the integers as a closed totality.
The process dictions familiar from other programming languages will replace such references, that
is, dictions that allow (possibly recursive)
sequential invocation of a set of basic processes
until a desired state is reached. Thus we can cook
up a language of two sets of ingredients -- partly
the static dictions of set theory, restricted,
however, to finite sets exclusively and partly the
*while*s, *go-to*s and *call*s from the programming
languages. In cooking, these two originally dis-
parate sets of elements will, of course, interpene-
trate each other.

To the basic reflections set forth above, we
may add certain fundamental observations concerning
programming languages. It is useful to classify
programming languages into two polar subtypes:
procedural languages and *object-describing languages*
(see reference 1). A programming language, if it
is not merely to be a syntactic format within which
certain standard services can be invoked, must embody
some interesting and useful "algebra" of complex
objects and a notation allowing these objects and
various operations combining them to be described.
Examples of such algebras are

     1. Arrays and their transformations, as in
APL;
     2. Strings, patterns, and various associated
operations, especially matching operations, as in
SNOBOL;
     3. General classes of objects interacting
through discrete events, as in SIMSCRIPT, SIMULA,
and GPSS;
     4. Elastic structures formed out of thin
members, and their interconnections, as in STRESS,
COGO, and various other engineering languages.

These examples (which might be multiplied) show
a progression from the most "procedural" type to the
most "object-describing" type of language.

Procedural languages serve to describe a universe of stored data objects and a certain algebra of transformations on these objects, the transformations being applicable in combination and iteratively. Object-describing languages serve to describe one or more data objects, to which certain implicitly understood algorithms will apply in a manner determined by the structure of the object. Generalizing from the examples given above, we may attempt to answer the question, What are programming languages? — a question evidently basic in any exploration of programming language design. I would like to suggest the following outlines of an answer: Programming languages are notational systems devised to facilitate the description of abstract objects whose basic elements are sets, mappings, and processes. Associated with these objects will be a well-defined rule for evaluating them; perhaps, since the objects may contain processes as subparts, it would be better to say, for interpreting them. From this point of view, procedural programming languages of the ordinary serial kind may be regarded as a mechanism for the description of a set of basic transformation blocks, with each of which is associated a family of possible successors. Each block must also be furnished with a "terminating conditional transfer," which can be used during interpretation of the program to select one potential successor block as the actual "point of transfer." Object-describing languages will depart strongly from this familiar kind of location-counter control, however. In simulation languages, for example, the basic principle of control is quite different: The subprocesses of a simulation naturally form an unordered set, each of which is furnished with an invocation condition. The simulation interpreter executes, in any order, all processes whose invocation condition is satisfied as long as any remain to be executed; when none remain, an underlying time-parameter is advanced by the interpreter, and the next cycle of simulation begins.

If we bear in mind this broad range of possibilities, we can sharpen our response to the question posed above as follows: The "front" or

Specification Language Design

"syntactic" part of a language system must provide methods by means of which very general abstract objects (graph-like rather than tree-like, i.e., admitting remote rather than purely local connections) can be described conveniently. This "front end" should be variable enough so that the descriptive notation to be used can be tailored to the requirements of any particular field, permitting the objects of most common concern in this field to be described in a succinct and heuristically comfortable manner. Powerful mechanisms for describing the diagnostic or verification tests to be applied to text during its syntactic analysis should also form part of this language-system front end. The "back" or interpreter part of a language system should incorporate abstract structures that are general enough so that all the structured objects that may be of concern in a particular situation can conveniently be mapped upon these structures.

The design of a language ought to begin with an exploration of the semantic universe to which the language is to relate and with an elucidation of all those constructions that are useful and "natural" in this universe. A syntactic representation convenient for the description of these constructions should then be elaborated.

The set-theoretic language envisaged above is intended to be "procedural" in the sense just explained; that is, it will in one or another manner represent the algebra of all transformations on a universe of stored finite sets. Keeping in mind this fundamental semantic intent, we may add significantly to our insight by making certain remarks belonging to a general theory of the *construction* of highly complex compound objects of any sort, remarks that will serve to clarify various syntactic issues to be faced in elaborating detailed programming language designs.

The development of a complex program, like the construction of any highly structured object, consists of a progression of steps that supply piece after piece of a total. For the total to be correct it is, of course, necessary that all these separate elements cohere correctly. Each element must therefore satisfy certain constraints. The set of all those constraints that affect the choice of a program element E may be called the *logical context* of E. Note that in typical programming situations logical context will be defined by a miscellany of restrictions, particularly the following:

1. Syntactic restrictions determined by the programming language being used and by any definitional extensions to the language that may be operative in a given context.

2. Semantic requirements reflecting particular properties of subprocesses (already defined or to be defined) that are to be invoked in a given context.

3. Semantic requirements related to the structure of the data objects to be manipulated in a given code section.

4. Accumulated odds and ends, as, for example, restrictions implied by the previous uses of particular data items, subroutine names, or so forth.

As noted, a program is built by choosing a sequence of elements, each correct in its logical context. The probability that a given element E will be correctly chosen will fall off rapidly with increasing complexity of its logical context, and, beyond a certain threshold T of complexity, this probability will effectively be zero. We may accordingly define a *programmable process* (and, more generally, a *constructible compound object*) as a process that can be realized by a program none of whose constituent elements need be chosen in a logical context whose complexity exceeds a complexity threshold T. One can expect to complete, in a time proportional to N, a program P of length N whose complexity of local context is everywhere bounded by a constant $T_1 < T$, but the presence within P of any extensive section whose local complexity exceeds T may make P impossible to complete.

These considerations show that in programming elaborate processes we must aim systematically to prevent the development of excessively complex local contexts.[1]

---

[1] One might elaborate an overall theory of a programming process along lines suggested by the remarks made above. Suppose that a total program P consists of elements $E_1, \ldots, E_n$ and that the local complexity of context of the element E_j is C_j. Then we suggest that the total effort required to complete the entire program P will be measured by
$$\text{tot}(P) = f(C_1) + \ldots + f(C_n)$$
where f is a function growing rapidly with C and becoming quite large at some finite complexity threshold T. A formula of this sort can account for various observed features of the programming process, including the very large fluctuations that the quantity tot(P) exhibits even when P remains fixed. (One group of programmers may complete a project many times more rapidly than another, even when both groups are involved with quite similar projects.) We take this to reflect the rapid growth of f(C) with C, a growth that would imply that relatively small increases in logical systematization, applied consistently, could have a substantial effect on the effort tot(P). The very large observed variations in individual programmer activity can similarly be derived from smaller individual variations in complexity tolerance.

The suggested formula for total programming efforts leads also to potentially useful insights concerning the development of a programming project during its lifetime. When an element E_j of a program is initially "sketched out," the logical complexity of its local context is momentarily elevated due to the fact that various still-to-be-resolved uncertainties concerning undeveloped elements of P form part of the initial logical context of E_j. We call this transitional element

Hence we shall need to invent mechanisms capable of preventing the propagation of complexity between sections of an extensive program. Having reference

---

in the context complexity of E_j *external irresolution complexity*. When the whole of a first draft of P is completed, this temporary contribution to local complexity disappears, ideally allowing the elements E_j to be confirmed (or revised as necessary) a good deal more surely and rapidly than they were first elaborated. A contrary force arises, however, from the fact that various details specified during the development of elements $E_1, \ldots, E_{j-1}$ (and especially those relating to data structures) become part of the context of E_j. We call this contribution to the context complexity of E_j *accumulated external complexity*. The accumulation of external complexity may cause projects to behave pathologically, the context complexity of key elements actually increasing over the life of the project, which may make project completion impossible or at least very much more tedious than initially estimated.

These last remarks suggest certain principles that might usefully be applied to determine the order in which the various parts of a complex project can most usefully be tackled.

1. The most complex elements of the project should be surveyed first, and the relationships of these elements to the remaining project elements (their "external environment") determined to a reasonable degree of approximation. Overall decisions concerning those aspects of the simpler project elements that form significant parts of the logical context of the more complex elements should then be taken. These decisions must, of course, be made tentatively but should be sufficiently firm and detailed to relieve the more difficult elements of most of their external irresolution complexity.

2. Full program development should then begin *with the most complex project elements*, which should

to the above remarks concerning the principal loci of context complexity, we see therefore that we must attempt to limit the influence within a program of

1. Complex invocable subprocesses

2. Internal structural details of complex data objects.

Since processes in procedural languages are transient but their effect on data objects carries forward, process definitions will normally not exert so pervasive a force as data structure definitions in propagating complexity. Of course, if inappropriate subprocesses are specified as standard, this can propagate complexity to remote contexts. Nevertheless, really virulent increases in the local complexity of a program will normally be traceable data-structure-related sources. Thus, to hold the complexity of local context within a program below a fixed limit, we must more than anything else standardize the data structures that the program uses.

---

be brought relatively far along before detailed work on the simpler project elements is taken up. Accumulated external complexity will then complicate only the simpler project elements; these increments to complexity have a less harmful effect than increases in the context complexity of already complicated elements might have.

Note also that the above considerations underscore the importance of breaking a complex project into smaller relatively independent pieces and of staging the project in a structured manner that allows the treatment of potentially complicating factors to be postponed when possible. Linguistic mechanisms that accord with this intent will be used in the SETL language in connection with whose design many of the principles reported in this paper have been developed.

The use of standardized data structures will imply a certain standardization of the processes that manipulate these structures. In particular, we will find it necessary to avoid the use of processes that can create structures of non-standard form. This restriction concerning processes to be used has then significant implications of its own. If, having decided on the use of certain standardized data structures, we ever make use of operations that transform these structures into non-standard forms, the non-standard details of these forms become part of the logical context of every instruction that might manipulate a non-standard structure. Complexity can build up very rapidly in such situations, and for this reason we will normally prefer to avoid them. Thus, once having chosen certain data structures for standard use, we will normally proceed at once to standardize a family of basic operators addressing these structures and to describe compound processes only (or almost only) in terms of the set of basic operators thus designated. The approach sketched here, which makes use of standardized data structures and of combinable basic operators affecting them, is that which lies at the basis of every programming language design. The standardization upon which we insist can, of course, have a negative effect on the efficiency that our method will attain in any particular case; and it is this consideration that may again and again tempt us to the use of more highly varying non-standard forms. Within the approach envisaged here, however, efficiency-enhancing non-standard variations are allowable only in a phase of programming subsequent to the initial layout, in terms of standardized elements, of a programming approach. By relegating efficiency-related design supplements and redesigns to a second stage of programming, we confine, to a limited set of specified contexts, a significant class of programming activities likely to propagate complexity. In particular, we become better able to avoid *inadvertent* decisions in particular contexts, which propagate complexity to other portions of a program; decisions of this kind can, when higher-level preplanning is absent or insufficiently detailed, have most unfortunate complexity-

propagation effects. Moreover, by thinking first
in terms of a standardized class of data structures,
and only subsequently of those concrete variations
that are truly desirable for increased efficiency,
we will often find that the range of variations
that must be made is smaller than could have been
realized at first, so that these variations can
themselves be standardized. In such cases, we will
be able to develop automatic optimization methods
that incorporate efficiency-enhancing variations
in programs written in languages of high level and
that produce programs that compare favorably to
those developed in lower-level languages by
programmers forced to function in contexts straining
their maximum complexity tolerance.

 A data structure S in which many processes
interface may itself tend to grow complex, and we
will therefore wish to prevent its full complexity
from affecting, to an unnecessary degree, the various
processes that must address it. We therefore wish
it to be possible for each process P to deal only
with those aspects of S that are of concern to P,
ignoring all others. That is, each process P should
be able to view S in whatever logical "projection"
is appropriate. To allow this we will wish P and
S to be linked via *access functions* that allow P
to reference those aspects of S that it must. Note
in particular that we find it desirable to represent
the necessary access operations explicitly, rather
than to represent them implicitly in coding patterns
to be used throughout P. In particular, those basic
attributes of S to be accessed and modified ought to
be explicitly named within P and not represented in
implicit fashion by compound access sequences;
mnemonic names, rather than numerical subpart addresses, should be used for attributes, etc. Explicit
linkage of programs to data also has various other
advantages.

 The emphasis that we have placed on the role
of data structures in determining certain of the
fundamental properties of programming languages that
address them suggests certain further points. A
programming language ought to incorporate powerful

methods for the definition of compound data forms and for the specification of new operations applying to and combining them. Appropriately specified semantics mechanisms that might perhaps be represented in a convenient way by external syntactic forms could facilitate the definition of operations on new data objects in terms of existing operations. Explicit mechanisms that allow operators to be related to the data structures on which they are to act should be provided.

In addition to the data-related issues treated above, various other ways in which language design can aid in limiting context complexity may be noted. Note, first, that by making decisions in separated stages whenever possible we can reduce the complexity level with which we must deal at any given time. This may be called the *principle of decision postponement*. In decision postponement lies one of the basic advantages of the use of specification languages and the "two-stage" programming style proposed in this note. Various more direct hints concerning language design may also be drawn from this principle. First, language should be able to treat semantically analogous entity classes, which may be substitutable for each other in a syntactically identical way, so that the decision concerning which type of entity is actually to be used can be postponed. It should also be possible to defer decisions concerning the manner in which a particular code section is to be used until after the code section is elaborated.

The inner details of a program section should be isolated to a maximum degree from detailed conventions determined by other program sections. This may be called the *principle of structural isolation*. Note in particular that semantically unitary items established outside a program element E should be represented within E by unitary names and not by complex sequences defined by external program sections.

Those items to whose details a given item E is most closely related should find places physically near E without distracting less closely related material being included. This may be called the *principle of grouping by logical relation*. In accordance with this principle we find it undesirable for a language to establish rigid conventions concerning the order in which syntactic elements must appear.

At NYU we are currently engaged in the design and initial implementation of a set-theoretic, procedural programming language designated SETL. Hopefully, this language will reflect the general design principles set forth above. (See reference 2 for a quite preliminary account of this language with some explorations of its use in the depiction of algorithms.)

The increasing disdain for new language that some of the most sophisticated computer scientists have expressed of late leads me to put the following question very directly:

Is it reasonable to expect that the definition and implementation of such a language will, merely because of the mathematicized character of the language and its systematic adaptation to the purpose of algorithm specification, create any advantages at all? I contend that the answer is yes, and I contend, moreover, that the benefits that such a language will provide are numerous and substantial. I buttress this claim by indicating one of the most general of the beneficial effects expected, an effect upon computer science education. The availability of a mathematicized programming language should in relatively short order lead to a restructuring of the way that computer science is taught.

Presently one begins with a basic course, titled variously but generally called something like Introduction to Data Structures and Algorithms. When an appropriate abstract specification language becomes available, this fundamental subject matter should fall into two parts, which might be separately called *abstract algorithmics* and *concrete algorithmics* Abstract algorithmics will be concerned with the depiction and analysis of complex algorithmic processes, independently of the way in which the logical objects to which they refer are to be mapped into a computer. Concrete algorithmics, on the other hand, will have the following as its problem: Given a family of abstract objects and processes that are to affect them, how can these objects best be mapped into tabular form and the associated processes actually carried out? Note that by isolating and first solving some of the problems of abstract algorithmics, we may expect to be able to discuss concrete algorithmic problems in a more satisfactory manner than has hitherto been typical. Before one knows what one wants to do in a complex situation, one is really not in a very good position to study the ways in which one might do it. Conversely, once an abstract algorithm is put forth, one is generally able to envisage a much wider range of concrete approaches to its optimization than would otherwise be possible. From the point of view of the present work, prior systematic attempts at the depiction of algorithms have generally failed to separate the abstract from the concrete parts of the algorithmic questions that they study but have mixed the abstract with the concrete, rather to the disadvantage of both. It may also be mentioned that it is abstract rather than concrete algorithmics that stand closest to a third principal branch of computer science, that which plays so large a role in Donald Knuth's magnificent series of books, namely the *formal performance analysis of algorithms*.

A second benefit is this: The succinctness and descriptive power of a mathematicized programming language will enable us to depict complex processes in their totality, in decisive detail, and in a form free of abstractly irrelevant specifics. Since our view of complex abstract algorithms will be total and detailed rather than fragmentary and vague, we will have a better chance to consider the form and effect of variations in our algorithms and the possible generalizations of them. Bringing the abstract kernel of a process out from behind the veil of abstract irrelevancies that normally obscure it, we will make this kernel more communicable and hence more capable of systematic rational discussion than would otherwise be the case. The elimination of irrelevant specifics from formally stated algorithms has still another substantial benefit. Specificity is a major source of incompatibility between algorithms, and abstractness will therefore enhance compatibility. Consider, for example, the problem of piecing together a compiler out of its customary principal components: parser, optimizer, code generator, etc. We find, typically for a whole class of similar situations, that across each of the interfaces between principal modules some collection, generally rather small, of structured data items must be passed. From the abstract point of view, these will be unproblematical enough: They may be trees, graphs, a few mappings defined thereupon, and so forth.

If one module will naturally produce trees or graphs, and another can conveniently accept such as an input, no serious problem of compatibility is to be expected at the abstract level, and separately written modules can readily be fitted into a totality. The situation immediately becomes different when abstract data structures are mapped into concrete tabular form. To do so is to define a host of pointer and indexing mechanisms, supplementary variables, overflow conventions and flags, special abbreviations relating to particular data subcases, field sizes, punctuations, and so forth. These definitions, precisely because from the abstract point of view they are largely arbitrary, will never be cast in precisely the same way for two separate program modules except by careful preplanning, and, of course, any deviation from perfect agreement may require data restructurings so complex and touchy as to be prohibitive. In this we have the case that generally makes it impossible to design useful program library components that will either accept complex data structures as input or provide such structures as output, unless, as is the case with the SETL specification language, a language of sufficient generality provides a fixed framework·of conventions. For this reason, intermodule data interfaces often become the foci of major difficulties during the design of large programming systems, wherein months are often consumed in negotiations concerning the detailed layout of data structures to be passed between principal modules. It is usually found in such situations that all the technical groups involved have elaborated their design ideas not abstractly but in terms of certain implicit assumptions concerning data layout, assumptions that, understandably enough, they become loath to give up. Moreover, no powerful algorithmic communication technique permitting one group to gain an understanding of the processes that the others are going to apply is available, so that the trade-off issues involved in the choice of data layouts tend to remain obscure on both sides. Naturally, it is then hard to come to intelligent technical compromises. The systematic pre-elaboration of algorithmic strategy using a powerful specification language should cast a welcome light on this dark and perilous corner.

Given that the elimination of irrelevant specifics will restrict the tendency toward incompatibility of program modules in a significant way, we may expect to be able to produce fairly complex standard formal algorithms adaptable for use in a variety of situations. Thus it should become possible to put larger items into the cabinet of prefabricated programs than have hitherto filled it. In reference 2 a start in this direction is made.

Yet a third anticipated benefit that we expect the use of a mathematicized specification language to provide is this. Our method allows the abstract specification of an algorithmic process to go forward to completion before any of the concrete table-and-code design issues connected with it have to be faced. When our language is implemented, it will even be possible to execute the abstract programs, and to verify their correctness experimentally. During this process a much smaller mass of program text will be involved than is now the case; it will be much more feasible than it now is to experiment with significant variations in approach during the development of an algorithm. Then, having a debugged

algorithm in hand, one will be able to survey it to
get a detailed picture of all the data structures
that it involves, of all their parts, and of all
the processes that must effect these parts. It
should then be easier than it is now to come
to sophisticated final decisions concerning the
table structures, data management strategies, and
code techniques to be used in a highly efficient
version of the same algorithm. In current practice,
both classes of issues, abstract design and concrete
layout, must be faced at once, and generally in a
situation of confusion in which a programmer, already
forced to cope with all the complexity that he can
juggle, may be unwilling even to contemplate promising optimizations if they threaten to add to the
mass of material that he must sustain. Moreover,
in typical current situations it is quite hard to
maintain design balance, with the consequence that
certain parts of the system may be overdesigned,
while others, equally or more crucial, may be sorely
neglected and their insufficiency discovered only
when it has become impossible, or at least extremely
expensive, to do anything about it. The algorithmic
language that we propose should, in short, allow
the full complex of program-design issues to be
approached in orderly stages and allow minor
matters to be classified as such, whereby design
attention can be concentrated to ferret out highly
effective solutions to key problems.

   Most of the benefits to which we have until now
alluded come from the use of a suitably powerful
specification language, independently of whether
this language is implemented. When the mathematicized programming language we project is available
for running, however, additional advantages will
accrue. A language of this kind cannot but be a
most appropriate tool for those situations,
especially characteristic of university programming,
in which experimental algorithms are developed to
be run a few times and then improved or discarded
after certain aspects of their behavior are observed.
A tool of this kind will also be useful when an
elaborate program needs to be built to run just
once, or when a complex program whose sole task is

to prepare tables for some other program must be
produced, or when meta-compilers or other large
programs of infrequent use must be prepared, etc.
The mathematician desiring to experiment with combinatorial situations but unwilling to make a very
heavy investment in programming will find a language of the type projected most welcome. The computer scientist will find that it allows him to
realize more elaborate algorithms than would otherwise be in reach. Such attractions have made APL
increasingly popular; I consider that the partly
set-theoretic nature of that ingeniously devised
array language lies at the root of this phenomenon.

In the development of large programming systems
within an industrial setting, a technique allowing
the rapid and inexpensive development of functioning,
even if inefficient, versions of complex programs
must also be of decided advantage for several
reasons. Presently, large-program development
suffers badly from the fact that little or nothing
begins to function visibly until a huge whole has
been brought far along. At this point, vast sums
may have been spent and time irrecoverably invested.
It is then generally the case that what is done is
done and that a project must either bull through
along a fixed course, whatever its internal or
external deficiencies, or die. Simply by shortening
the perilously long feedback loops that characterize
present development techniques, an executable
specification language would prove of great advantage.

It may also be remarked that during the development of a large system substantial expenses are
occasioned by the fact that in such projects it is
often necessary to write masses of scaffold-code
against which developing systems components can be
tested. Intending that our mathematicized specification language should obviate this, we have been
at pains to specify an interface linking the specification language to a conventional field-manipulation language of the kind that would normally be
used for systems programming. In tandem with such
a "lower-level" language, our specification language can act as a test-case generator.

The full development of this idea leads to what might be called a two-stage development technique. The first of the two programming stages consists of the development and debugging of a complete systems algorithm, written in the abstract language, and the annotation of this algorithm with all those remarks concerning intended concrete techniques and data management strategy necessary to define the detailed program that is to be developed during the second stage. This first programming stage will also involve measurement and user testing, wherein the abstract algorithm serves as a kind of detailed simulator of the efficient program that it foreshadows and wherein it may be modified as necessary During the second stage of programming, all the parts of an abstract code are progressively replaced with logically equivalent but much more efficient passages of concrete code, which are hammered out against the abstract algorithm.

All plans involving execution of abstract specification languages must eventually hope to demonstrate that, even though the efficiency losses that the highly generalized standardization of data representations must occasion will be large, they need not be catastrophic. Loss factors of 10, or even of 100, can be borne; loss factors of 1000 (which we do not at all anticipate) would be disastrous. Technology has, after all, increased memory capacities by a factor of 100, and speeds by even larger factors, over the last dozen years and promises to continue making similarly spectacular gains. Would it not for many purposes be clearly worthwhile to go back a generation in machines if by doing so we could increase by a large factor our ability to program?

As a final benefit, we expect the availability of a mathematicized algorithm specification language to broaden the frontier of contact between programming and mathematics. It should at any rate serve to emphasize to the mathematician that programming need not be a mass of petty detail only, that in fact it is concerned, in a way only slightly unfamiliar, with some of the issues that he is accustomed

to confronting, that interesting inductive proofs
can in fact be regarded as recursive algorithms, and
so forth.

   While the mathematician will presumably find
a mathematically oriented language like that we
propose more familiar, and hence more accessible,
than customary programming languages might be, the
programmer coming to it with a conventional background will find it necessary to change certain of
his central habits, and this may at first be rather
disconcerting. Conventionally, the mental process
of program elaboration that eventually results in
a finished program design or program begins not only
with half-formulated procedure kernels but as much
as anything else with some idea of the data
structures that are to support the procedures to
be employed. Often enough the first part of a total
design that appears on paper is an initial elaboration of these data structures, their fields,
and the separate significances of these fields.
This data depiction is conventionally used as an
anvil against which all the detailed processes that
eventually will form part of a complete package are
shaped. From the present point of view, all this —
ingrained habit of the most skillful programmers
though it is — is defective, since it indiscriminately
confounds the abstract essentials of a process to be
described with a host of matters of quite different
character. The procedure we suggest is different.
Bypassing very much of this customary matter, or at
the very least making it a postscript to rather than
the start of our specification process, we deal
not with *tables*, *fields*, and *pointers*, but directly
with those *logical associations*, *correspondences*,
and *sets* that conventional tabular data structures
ultimately and indirectly represent. The sudden
loss of burden that so radical a simplification
implies may at first be somewhat disorienting, and
the new medium may at first seem too rarefied to
breathe. Nevertheless, the necessary new habits of
thought are in fact readily acquired and, once
mastered, can lead to a substantial improvement in
one's ability to design eminently practical algorithms. But the necessary design steps will be taken

in quite a different order.

APPENDIX I: ADDITIONAL REMARKS CONCERNING THE FUTURE DEVELOPMENT OF PROCEDURAL LANGUAGES

Although the statement of an algorithm in the SETL language alluded to above is now often shorter than a natural language description of the same algorithm, the natural-language descriptions are nevertheless generally clearer in a somewhat elusive but still real sense. This suggests that natural language embodies useful descriptive mechanisms that SETL still has not captured and that ought to be sought after. This appendix contains a few preliminary observations in this direction.

1. A very important feature of natural-language discourse lies in the fact that such discourse is highly error-tolerant. That is, numerous small deviations from standard grammar, of the kind that lead to such irritations in programming, are automatically corrected in normal discourse. In programming situations, one may allow error correction to be applied during a parse, but one is normally reluctant to allow an automatic scheme for the correction of syntactic errors to be followed by execution. The essential reason for this lies in the fact that once execution begins all feeling for the reasonableness of computation is lost, the computer in no real way monitoring the overall progress of its actions. In particular, even if an error might have been corrected in one of several ways, one will be chosen, and it will then not be possible to detect the fact that the computation that results is unreasonable and that an alternative correction, leading to a different calculation, ought to be tried. These considerations emphasize the importance of various potential features of programming languages:

a. If the programmer's assumptions concerning his program are made available, then not only are useful static error checks possible, but one may become considerably more willing to go ahead with program execution after error correction. In addition to the "assume" type of statement discussed in [3] (p. 10), statements that indicate the expected length of loops, the expected pattern of control transitions in a program, and so forth, might all be useful.

   b. Error-correction mechanisms ought to interact much more intelligently with static global program analysis procedures (of the kind involved in optimization) than is now the case. For example, spelling-error-correction procedures could focus on variables live on program entry (improperly initialized variables) that are particularly likely to be misspelled versions of other variables, especially if there existed variables with similar spellings that had explicit definitions whose results were never used. Likewise, undefined functions are suspect as misspelled data objects, etc.

   These remarks serve to emphasize the great importance of diagnostic aids in the programming process. Mechanical aids, such as selective text retrievals and partial program analyses, which aim at increasing a programmer's maximum toleration for local complexity, are also desirable. It would, for example, be quite useful to be able to request display of all uses of a given assignment.

   c. Beyond the relatively straightforward issues raised above we come to the whole area of logical consistency checks in a higher sense. It is probably not possible to penetrate far into these matters now, though, of course, they deserve determined investigation.

   2. Another important fact concerning natural language discourse, and one that it may be possible to exploit in a formal-language setting, is the fact that natural language makes clever use of syntactic ambiguities, which are then resolved by fragments of semantic information available from preceding declarations and inferences. For example,

Specification Language Design 25

in natural language one may say

α: "Proceed in increasing order through the elements a of a sequence s. If a exceeds the element b that succeeds it, then interchange a and b."

The most desirable translation of this into a formal language would be something like the following (we write in a syntactic style corresponding to SETL):

β: "*sequence* s; (∀ a ε s) if a *gt* nextafter(a) (callthis b), then <a,b> = <b,a>; ..."

where the first statement is a declaration. But instead we are compelled to write (in the present version of SETL)

γ: "(1 < ∀n < #s) if s(n) *gt* s(n+1) then <s(n), s(n+1)> = <s(n+1),s(n)>; ..." .

In the last statement, a distracting position counter, which natural-language manages to suppresss, has become explicit; also, the next element after a is referenced using the explicit definition of successor in a sequence rather than in terms of the logical relationship this successor bears to a, as in natural language.

The observed differences come ultimately from the fact that various bits of semantic information concerning the notion "sequence," as, for example, the fact that elements of a sequence may be thought of as having both a value a(n) and a position n, are not capable of being exploited when the code γ is written. This has the consequence that a considerable measure of local complexity absent in the hypothetical code β appears in γ.

Consider what is necessary to make a programming style such as β possible. We must first have some way of handling the basic declaration "*sequence* s;," which, somewhat in the manner of a macro, must give us the information needed to make all those deductions and transformations that are subsequently necessary, which are roughly as follows:

1. Since a appears in the context a ε s, we see that this name is being used for a "sequence element" (this involves an "implicit declaration").

2. Iteration over a sequence is known to involve its elements in order and is really the indices of these elements. Thus (∀x ε a) is seen to be a shorthand for (1 < ∀n < #s), where "n" is a position pointer, attached implicitly to "a"; certain subsequent uses of "a" will really be references to n.

3. nextafter(a) is probably an elliptical reference to the sequence element a(n+1) (or to its position); this inference could fail only if there were some other attribute of a (as perhaps its value, if this value were an integer) that could be incremented.

Note in this connection that in natural language a name is used ambiguously for a group of associated object attributes and that the question of how an operation is to be applied to the name is resolved by considering which particular attribute can logically be an argument of the operation. Among other advantages, this manner of using names has the advantage of making explicit certain helpful logical associations between items that programming languages tend to pretend are unrelated. Such a use of names also serves to hide the details of accessing sequences that use a known value of one attribute to select the corresponding value of another attribute. For example, in β there is nothing corresponding to the explicit indexing operation s(n). This small effect can, of course, become quite large when data structures more complex than sequences are being addressed.

4. Since there would be no point in applying the "comparison" operator *gt* if the positions n and n+1 were the objects of reference, the first uses of a and b in β must refer to values and not locations,

that is, to "s(n)" and "s(n+1)," respectively.
Similarly, since an assignment operation must be
"indexed," the form

$$<s(n),s(n+1)> = <s(n+1),s(n)>$$

implied by

$$<a,b> = <b,a>$$

of β can be deduced.

We may in summary list certain of the principal
logical elements that would have to enter into the
design of a "reasoning" compiler capable of accepting inputs such as β. Rather than treating tokens
as undifferentiated "names" after the fashion of
current compilers, such a compiler would have to
associate specific attributes, with tokens used to
represent variables. Some of these attributes could
be explicitly declared; others would have to be
deduced from the contexts in which the tokens were
used. The manner in which a text fragment was to
be expanded would depend not only on the keywords
present in a text but also on the attributes of
the tokens that it contained. (Note that the
"attribute-dependent macro expansion" style that
this suggests is not standard.) In this way, by
using a single name to represent various mutually
associated attributes, we recreate within a programming language the vital natural-language notion of
"object." This enables us to hide from view all the
detailed code that, given one or more attributes
of an object, accesses its other attributes.

We see from the preceding that ambiguity is
exploited in various ways in natural language.
Among other things, it allows a type of decision
postponement. This suggests that the use of a
parsing style well adapted to handle syntactic
ambiguities might be appropriate to programming
languages also and that the development of ambiguity-tolerant parsers could be a useful first step
toward "reasoning" parsers of the kind that we have
projected.

APPENDIX II: WHAT IS PROGRAMMING?

The general principles set forth in the preceding pages allow us to elaborate a series of answers to the pregnant question, What is programming.

1. To start with, *programming is the activity that builds the interface between man, on the one hand, and computers, on the other*. Certain of its characteristics will then be determined by man and others by the computer. The goal of programming is the construction of advanced function, which requires the perfection of complex programs. Therefore

2. *Programming is the process of constructing complex objects*. In the preceding pages, certain basic laws affecting such processes of construction were outlined. To repeat, compound objects are built by successive correct choices of a sequence of elements $E_1,\ldots,E_n$. Each element E_j must be chosen in a logical context that summarizes all those aspects of other elements that are relevant to the choice of E_j. We call the collection of all these influences the *local context* of E_j, and call any reasonable numerical measure of this collection the *context complexity* of E_j. It may then be observed that the chance of choosing E_j correctly falls off very rapidly as its context complexity increases, and effectively becomes zero at a not very large threshold T. This observation allows us to define the class of *constructible objects*: an object is constructible if it can be built by choosing elements successively, each in a context of complexity less than T. A function is programmable if it can be realized by a program that is constructible.

To construct a large object successfully, one must therefore combine many subelements. The rules according to which elements may be combined are, of course, part of the logical context of every element. These rules must therefore be simple. But a simple set of rules allowing the indefinitely iterated combination of simple elements into a large totality defines some sort of "algebra." Therefore

3. *Programming constructs compound objects from simpler elements by combining elements according to the rules of some "algebra."*

To program, therefore, one must be aware of some such algebra, which must be capable of generating objects representing useful processes. Before they can be used, such algebras must be found. We conclude therefore that in a deeper sense

4. *Programming is the discovery of algebraic principles allowing the iterated combination of elements into compound objects representing useful processes.*

Next, observe that although the maximum threshold T of tolerable complexity postulated above will vary from person to person, for no one person is it very large. In this regard a group of people is no better than a single person. Therefore an object not constructible in the above sense can really never be constructed directly, either by individuals or by large teams. And it is very unlikely that such an object will be formed spontaneously by the action of a random process, even if this process acts repeatedly over long periods of time. Objects irreducibly unconstructible must therefore remain nonexistent. The barrier to their existence should be as firm as those set for mathematics by theorems of the type of Gödel.

There is, however, a way in which we can hope to find a way around the obstacle revealed by these pessimistic reflections. To see this, observe that the maximum context complexity of the elements of a compound object is by no means independent of the representation of the object. What in one representation may appear as a densely interconnected mass will in another representation appear as an object, perhaps still large, but consisting constructibly of items no group of which **are** impenetrably related.

To discover this second representation of a programming problem is to break the problem's back, since this discovery allows one to build what formerly were obscurely integral objects using systematic incremental techniques, that is, to proceed by the progressive accumulation of tables of information possessing no overwhelming degree of internal interconnectedness. In a still higher sense, therefore,

    5. *Programming is the discovery of viewpoints or logical transformations that uncover hidden algebras in terms of which compound objects representing useful processes may be built. That is, programming is simplification, and, like mathematics, is a hunt for lucky simplifications.*

It is worth emphasizing that the discovery of these simplifications is the essential goal of experimental, as distinct from applied, programming. If in a strictly research situation we build a highly compound object, we do so only in the hope that immersion in the realities of a particular construction process may put us in mind of principles allowing this process to be simplified.

The transformation of a constructible compound object into that more highly interwoven form in which it directly represents some interesting function plainly amounts to a kind of *compilation*. (The practical possibility of carrying out such transformations is, of course, the contribution of the machine to the process of programming, which, in the preceding remarks, we have viewed almost exclusively from the human side of the man-machine interface.) We may therefore say that

    6. *Programming is the discovery of algebras allowing the construction of objects worth compiling and is the programming of compilers for these objects.*

Elements that programmers are to combine need to be simple externally. But, as long as their internal complexity can be hidden, they need not be simple internally. Indeed, when objects having simple external description but embodying powerful function can be allowed within an organized algebra, the programmer's reach is multiplied. Hence

   7. *Programming is the discovery of highly functional logical entity types possessing simple external descriptions and thus capable of being integrated into an algebra useful for the construction of still higher functions and is the discovery of the "internal" algebras that allow the construction of entities of these types.*

   The above remarks predicate an indirect method for creating functioning machine-level process representations. Our reflections concerning context complexity suggest that in the construction of highly compound objects such an indirect approach is inevitable. However, since this approach is, to begin with, fixed upon simplification and standardization as goals, in following it we run the risk of ignoring alternative constructions that might realize a given function in a particularly efficient way. Efficiency-oriented departures from a standardized approach are traditionally the prerogative of skilled human programmers. The mind, ranging analytically, can incorporate very useful variations into a basic approach, as long, that is, as the additional complications that such departures cause do not carry one over the threshold T of allowable context complexity. The programming range that we contemplate will, however, involve transformations of form so repeated and elaborate as to exclude the possibility of external meddling with the compiled versions of objects. Given that we will have to allow efficiency-enhancing variations to enter into the compilation process, it follows that in the programming range we contemplate it will be found necessary to systematize these variations and to build a *program* capable of weaving them into the compiled version of an initial text. Such a program must, of course, be able to analyze programs in sophisticated global ways. The programmer may assist this optimizer by adding, to a text to be compiled, disjointed declarations that summarize and transmit significant conclusions concerning the text, but his role may not safely be allowed to exceed this limit. We may in this regard say that

8. *Programming is optimization, that is, is the programming of optimizers able to analyze and improve other programs and is the discovery of principles that allow the simplification of such optimizers.*

The use of the indirect technique suggested above, involving the optimizing compilation of sequences of constructible objects, will eventually allow functions that lie utterly beyond the scope of more primitive direct methods to be programmed. Nevertheless, just as Gödel's theorem assures us that certain rather simple questions lie quite out of the range that the method of mathematical proof can reach, so we may also take it that certain functions that might be of great use are not programmable in that no constructible object can represent them, even after compilation. It is therefore of interest to consider whether the construction of artificial intelligences is at all possible. Might it not be that, among all those objects constructible within the maximum complexity threshold T of the human mind, none exists that can represent all the capacities of the mind?

In coming to grips with this question, one must first of all realize that it concerns innate and not learned capacities. That which is learned is drawn from an accumulation of separately encountered facts, presented in no particular order or relationship. No inextricably interwoven object is immediately represented in the pile of fragments presented as input to the learning process. If facts within the mind are interwoven in uncompilably complex ways, they can be so only because the mind is innately capable of establishing exceedingly complex connections. If the ability to learn can be programmed, the teaching process will be trivial. That which we seek to duplicate is therefore as fully present in the neolithic savage as in the *savant*.

But might not this innate facility, in spite of the somewhat restrictive definition that the above remarks give it, still be unprogrammable? It might. But I doubt that it is. Hard evidence in this area is still missing. To argue from what has not been done, or from the collapse of inflated initial projections, is an absurdity, given that the computer is still less than twenty-five years old. It seems to me that the fragmentary evidence that does exist ought to incline one rather strongly against such arguments. Substantial progress toward the programming of mental function has been made in a few cases. For example, the parser-compiler type of program captures a striking part of the ability to learn languages. Note that, in accordance with the general principles stated above, it is the discovery of an underlying algebra, specifically the algebra of pattern combination in the manner embodied in BNF grammars, that enables us to construct such programs.

One may conjecture that mental faculties that, like the ability to learn languages, are generalized and involve explicit learning will prove to be more readily constructible than faculties, such as visual pattern analysis, that are more rigidly fixed. Learning at the level of language learning is surely of late evolutionary arrival, and one may therefore surmise that this faculty has not had the time to grow as complex as have others. In view of the general pattern that evolution exhibits with regard to physical organs, we may take another hint from this observation. Speech and higher reasoning, rapidly evolved, may possibly employ specially adapted versions of faculties that antedate them. If this is true, then successful duplication of the mind's language-handling faculty may provide clues valuable for the analysis of still other mental functions.

The optimistic remarks of the preceding paragraph, if they can be trusted, lead one to try to put the question of artificial intelligence quantitatively. The programmability of a complex function is, as we have seen above, defined by the battery of simplifying transformations that determine one's programming technique. How many as yet undiscovered simplification principles remain to be found before artificial intelligences will, in this sense, become programmable? If and when these principles become available, how large a body of compilable text will be required to define the intelligence? I emphasize again that the text in question is that which organizes the intelligence's capacity to learn, not that possibly larger body of text that defines the total mass of facts available to it. That is, an intelligence is defined by those highly integral programs that determine the principles according to which it organizes more disjointed information tables subsequently fed to it. It would be rash to try to answer the questions just raised. Nevertheless, putting them serves, when one notes the extent to which a simple yet well-organized programming system such as LISP makes is possible to define quite striking language processing faculties by quite a small body of text, to buttress optimism. Putting these questions also serves to emphasize the central importance, for the eventual construction of artificial intelligences, of progress in programming technique. They also tell us what to look for: transformations that allow originally integral functions to be represented incrementally and in this sense to become learnable. Thus, for example, we may recognize that the organization of at least part of the language-analysis function around an explicit Backus algebra of syntactic patterns is a very significant step, the sort of thing that we must energetically seek to extend. Other functions can be cited for which organizing "algebras" are desirable and might be possible. An associational "feature noticing" function of a generalized sort would be useful in a wide variety of situations, for example in optimization by the method of "special cases," where such a mechanism might permit the easy addition of new optimizations. At a more technical level, a language of memory management, allowing certain central problems of concrete algorithmics to be treated systematically, could enhance our ability to produce efficient versions of concrete algorithms rapidly.

In connection with this last remark we may

raise yet another quantitative question concerning artificial intelligence. The capacity of an intelligence is measured both by the level of function that its responses embody and by the speed with which these responses can be generated. Assuming that it becomes possible to construct an intelligence, how fast will this intelligence be able to think? This question touches on all those questions of efficiency that, by concentrating on abstract programming issues in our preceding remarks, we have neglected. Its answer will, of course, be determined both by the basic capacities of the hardware available at a future date and by the extent to which optimization is able to overcome the natural tendency to inefficiency of a highly compiled programming style. Until now, almost all the most dramatic increases in program speed have come from basic hardware speedups. In a few cases, as with the development of the fast Fourier transform, fast sorts, hashing, and list-organized search techniques and the improvement of certain little-used combinatorial algorithms, programming has made similar contributions to efficiency. The domination of efficiency by hardware should continue for at least a while longer, as clock cycles diminish toward 10 nanoseconds and especially as improved manufacturing processes weaken the I/O barrier by making greatly expanded electronic memories available. In this regard programming may for a while have the largely subsidiary role of choosing algorithms that bypass potential combinatorial disasters. A more systematic but perhaps less immediately significant contribution of programming to efficiency will probably come through the continued development of optimization methods, especially those that, like cross-subroutine optimizations, aim at preventing the efficiency losses that a naive and highly compiled programming technique would imply.

Efficiency loss through the use of such techniques is in fact far from being a crucial problem. It has generally been true that, once able to organize a given programming area clearly, one has also been able to invent systematic optimizations that permit indirect programming techniques to attain an efficiency comparing not badly with results obtained by the use of much more expensive and eventually quite impractical manual techniques. In regard to the programming of intelligence, it may also be remarked that, once we are able to create a faculty, we may expect to be able to improve its efficiency substantially by providing it not in the most general form possible but in a specialized, "reflex-like" rather than fully "adaptable" form.

As the simplifying techniques needed to organize complex functions are progressively revealed through the progress of programming, the significance for efficiency of those elementary subprocesses exercised most constantly by the compiled form of programs written using these techniques will become plain. By realizing such "inner" subprocesses in hardware, one improves their efficiency through the elimination of unnecessary generality and by that use of large-scale parallelism that gives such great advantages to hardware realizations. An example of the type of situation we have in mind is currently seen in the tendency to simplify programming by speaking in terms of extremely large "virtual" memories. Such an approach makes certain simple "memory-mapping" operations of constant use and has led to the construction of these functions in hardware. Similar future influences of programming concept on hardware design are to be expected.

Artificial intelligences, if realized, will take programming as one of their first tasks, and it is interesting to try to guess the effect that this might have on programming. One of the great advantages of such intelligences will be their enormously large complexity tolerance, as compared to the capacity of the natural mind. In connection with the remarks made above we surmise that this will greatly extend the class of programmable functions, though in what way is not clear. Certainly, however, they should be capable of optimizing programs to a degree impossible to the natural mind and in this way can contribute substantially to their own development in efficiency.

REFERENCES

[1] Schwartz, J. T., "Semantic Definition Methods and the Evolution of Programming Languages," *Courant Computer Science Symposium 2: Formal Semantics of Programming Languages*, pp. 1-24, Prentice-Hall, 1972.

[2] ———, *Abstract Algorithms and a Set-Theoretic Language for Their Expression*, Preliminary draft, Computer Science Department, Courant Institute of Mathematical Sciences, New York University, 1971.

[3] ———, "An Overview of Bugs," *Courant Computer Science Symposium 1: Debugging Techniques in Large Systems*, pp. 1-16, Prentice-Hall, 1972.

DECLARATIVE AND EXTENDABLE LANGUAGES

Malcolm C. Harrison
Courant Institute of Mathematical Sciences
New York University

The requirements of a language for algorithm specification include conciseness; often obtained by the use of a special-purpose notation tailored to the application area. Thus the specification language should be extendable by the user. We describe a mechanism for extendability that gives the user considerable control over the translation process. In particular, it permits the specification of the complex processing that is necessary to translate declarative languages.

The development of high-level programming languages over the last decade has had a number of objectives, the most important of which has been the improvement of the efficiency of the programming process, which can, roughly speaking, be identified with the reduction of the time required to write and debug a program. In most cases there have been constraints on the type of improvements that could be made. These arose out of the requirement that the programming language execute efficiently, with a comparison frequently being made between the execution time of a program written in the high-level language and the same program written in assembly language.

However, in other areas, particularly those involving experimental programming in which a program is executed only a few times before it is modified, or in the case of highly complex programs that cannot be written except in a high-level language, the importance of fast execution times is much diminished. As machines have become faster and cheaper, and the complexity of algorithms has increased, convenience of use has become an increasingly important criterion for choosing a language, and execution speed has become less important. At the same time, an increasing knowledge of methods for doing optimization in compilers has enabled more powerful languages to compete in efficiency of execution with assembly-language programs.

The extreme type of language from this point of view is one in which the question of efficiency is ignored completely. Study of such languages is of some interest because it permits the consideration of languages in their purest roles as specifiers of algorithms. In addition it is possible to consider those attributes of languages that are concerned with matching the design of the language to the way of thinking of the programmer.

It would be generally agreed that one of the properties of such an "ideal" language would be simplicity. This term is often used to refer to a number of different things, including the following:

1. Ease of writing.
2. Ease of understanding.
3. Conciseness.

Measurement of the first two types of simplicity is clearly subjective and depends considerably on the programmer or reader, so it is apparent that agreement on a definition of this form of simplicity is not very likely. We all have our own ideas of what is easy to write and understand, and these ideas tend to be self-reinforcing as long as we are able to continue gaining facility in the language of our choice. It is possible to find advocates of a number of languages who will insist that their choice is

Declarative and Extendable Languages 41

the best; LISP, SNOBOL, APL, and ALGOL 68 enthusiasts come immediately to mind.

A more fruitful area for discussion is therefore the third measure of simplicity, conciseness. A crude but perfectly defensible measure of this is the number of symbols constituting the program. Some languages use large character sets that enable their programs to look smaller, but this is clearly of little theoretical significance. A better measure is perhaps the number of lexical tokens in the program.

Let us consider briefly some of the other methods that have been used to make programming language more concise. An important one is that which permits the programmer to eliminate repetitive code. This appears in a number of forms, including the procedure definition, which happily is also useful in reducing the amount of memory required by a program. Another form is the macro, which permits similar sections of code to be written only once. At first sight it might appear that declarations also contribute to conciseness, since they permit the elimination of code necessary for doing conversions between data types. But in fact this is not always true: the declarations are usually there to help the compiler produce better code, but the same logical effect can often be obtained by considering the data objects of the language as carrying their types with them and by doing run-time testing and conversion.

Another approach that languages have used to get conciseness is the provision of more powerful operators. This is seen in a primitive way in the MAP-type functions of LISP, and more significantly in the pattern-matching operations of SNOBOL and the generalized array operations of APL.

Perhaps the most effective way of shortening a program is to write it in a special-purpose language in which the basic data objects and operators are appropriate for the algorithm being considered. This approach has led to the development of numbers

of special-purpose programming languages, each with
a set of features that have been found useful in a
particular area of application. These features are
usually not compatible with each other, so it is
not possible to build a language with all of them
incorporated. In the simple cases in which this
can be done, such as PL/1, the result is a large
and cumbersome language.

In this paper we will consider two particular
ways of achieving conciseness in special-purpose
languages — declarative languages and extendable
languages.

EXTENDABLE LANGUAGES

The growth in number and variety of special-
purpose languages, many of which have many attributes
in common, has led to an interest in the development
of languages that can be tailored by the user to
his requirements. These are called extensible or
extendable languages and usually consist of a "core"
languages that possesses a minimum number of essential properties, together with a mechanism for
extending the language by definition of special-
purpose facilities in terms of those of the core
language.

The simpler forms of extendability, described
below, can be provided by preprocessing the text of
the program, which is a relatively easy technique
to implement. Accordingly, it is surprising that
the development of extendable languages has been so
slow. It seems likely that the responsibility for
this lies in the unsuitability of the earlier
algebraic languages such as FORTRAN and ALGOL 60
for use as core languages. More recently, it has
become apparent that these deficiencies are in the
area of data structures and storage allocation and
in the area of expressions, statements, and procedures. Roughly speaking, the first basic requirement for a core language is that the programmer be
able to specify an arbitrary operation the accessible

data at any point in the program by the insertion
of appropriate code at that point. This implies
that he is able to write commands in other commands
or in expressions and to create arbitrary data
structures or procedures. Furthermore, there is a
general requirement that such insertions, which may
be made by the extendability mechanism rather than
by the programmer directly, should not require
related modifications to be made in other parts of
the program. In this light, an otherwise rather
powerful language such as PL/1 appears quite
unsuitable. For example, it is not possible to
insert a command within an expression or to allocate memory for a data structure without concern
over the code to free this memory, possibly at a
quite different point in the program. An important
property of an extendable language is the way in
which the extensions are specified. Clearly, the
less the programmer has to know about the language
or the translator, the more convenient will be the
specification of the extensions. Thus while any of
the so-called compiler-compiler systems available
can be regarded as providing powerful facilities
for extending a language, their specification is
usually made in terms of modifications to the compiler tables, which require considerable knowledge
of the compiler as well as the language.

   Accordingly, the preferred method for specification of extensions of the language is in terms of
the language itself. Unfortunately the power of
the language that can be defined simply in this
way is highly dependent on the characteristics of
the core language. For example, it seems clear that
however powerful the extendability features for a
language such as FORTRAN, the specification of
extensions to provide the facilities of, say, ALGOL
60 would not be trivial. There seems to be a certain
"critical mass" that a core language requires to be
readily extendable.

   It is the apparent incompatibility between the
requirements for simplicity and power that is one
of the main problems of extendable-language design.
The language should be designed with enough hooks

in it to permit the user to use whatever knowledge
he has of the system to extend the language, so that
the knowledgeable user can modify the language in
significant ways, perhaps even by re-writing some
of the major translation routines. At the same time
the novice user should be able to make simple extensions easily, which requires the provision of a
convenient and easily understood form for specifying
the extensions. In this paper we suggest that a
convenient way of providing this facility is by
making the language used to specify the extensions
itself extendable.

EXTENDABILITY MECHANISMS

There have been a number of schemes proposed
to permit a language to be extended. If we consider
the translation process of a language to be divided
into three phases, namely

      1. Lexical scan,
      2. Syntax Analysis, and
      3. Code generation,

we can divide the types of extendability to be
classified according to the phase during which they
operate. A simple type of extendability is string
substitution, which is done prior to the lexical scan
phase. This takes the form of replacing a string
that matches a pattern with another string, which
may be a function of the original string. In the
simplest form the substituted string starts with a
keyword, but in the more powerful cases any string
matching a specified pattern will be substituted.
This type of extendability can be conveniently done
by passing the text through a program written in
some string-manipulation language such as SNOBOL.

Somewhat more power can be obtained by operating the string substitution in conjunction with
the lexical scan, thus restricting the components
that can be recognized to lexical units. This is
the mechanism used by PL/1, together with a general

string-processing subset of PL/1, which can be used to specify the transformation of the selected strings.

The difficulty with string substitution at the lexical scan level is that the transformation does not take into account the context in which the substitution is made.

A more powerful form of extendability is that which operates in conjunction with the syntax analysis phase. The idea is that the programmer should be able to define new forms of expressions or statements by specifying new syntactic forms and their translation. The syntax extensions are usually rather straightforward. In the case of a translator driven by a BNF-type syntax this can be done simply by permitting the user to specify new definitions. For example, if <x> is a syntactic type of the language, a new alternative form of <x>, which might be defined as

<x>   ::= <p><q><r>

may be added.

There may be problems if the new definition makes the language ambiguous, which cannot be determined by the translator in the general case. Accordingly, it is preferable to use a translator that will accept an ambiguous grammar (such as the Earley parser), which will give diagnostics only when it encounters an ambiguous program. Alternatively, the translator may be restricted to a subclass of the context-free languages for which there is an algorithm for determining ambiguity. There are also advantages to translators that can operate directly from the syntax information without extensive preprocessing.

A more difficult problem is that of specifying how the extensions should be translated. This is not surprising, since it is similar to the more general problem of specifying the semantics of a programming language, for which there appears no

satisfactory solution. However, it is simpler in
the sense that if the core language has the appropriate properties, the extensions can be stated
rather simply in terms of it rather than in terms
of any intermediate language or machine language.
The general mechanism then requires the translator
to recognize the syntax of the new language component and to replace it by the appropriately transformed version written in the core language. If
this new form is also an <x>, as is most likely,
this replacement can be done by simply modifying
the syntax tree, without further involvement of the
parser. It is also possible to specify a transformation of <p><q><r> without requiring that this
be identified as a particular syntactic type.

Of course, when more elaborate extensions are
required, such simple replacement procedures may be
either clumsy, inefficient, or impossible. In
that case it seems necessary to have the ability to
fall back on a general method for processing the
output of the parser, one that will allow the user
to specify arbitrary transformations of the syntax
tree as conveniently as possible. This has the
disadvantage of requiring a more detailed knowledge
of the workings of the translator, but there seems
to be no real alternative.

A particularly simple form of language that
has been found to be very suitable for extension is
the operator precedence language. This is always
unambiguous, can be extended in many useful ways
just by the definition of new operators together
with their precedences, and can produce a uniform
syntax tree that can be processed very simply.
The extendability features of ALGOL 68, perhaps the
best known of the extendable languages, are based
on an operator precedence grammar. A useful feature
of ALGOL 68 in this respect is the fact that operators and procedures are dependent on the types of
their arguments, which permits a form of context
dependence that is often useful.

DECLARATIVE LANGUAGES

The majority of programming languages are what are usually referred to as "imperative" languages. That is, they are most conveniently regarded as commands to the computer to carry out a certain sequence of operations. This is illustrated by the fact that in many programming languages many of the (erroneously called) "statements" are classified as "executable."

However, an increasing number of special-purpose application languages differ from the imperative languages in that their components are not imperative statements but declarative statements. Such statements are used not to direct the computer to execute some operation but to provide information to the translator about the properties of some object being considered. For the programmer, this can be useful in a number of ways. First, he sometimes does not know how to solve the problem and uses the translator as a black box that can solve it for him. This is particularly useful in applications areas in which the users are not familiar with the use of computers. Second, it permits him to specify only those things he is concerned with. He is often not interested in the way in which this object is represented in memory or the method that is used to solve his problem, and he is quite happy to leave these things up to the translator. That is, he knows how the computer will solve his problem but does not want to be concerned with the details. In some cases a detailed specification of his problem would in fact over-specify it, in the sense that he would be describing not the problem but a way of solving it. The translator may be able to solve the problem in the optimum way it is posed without unnecessary constraints.

The distinction between imperative languages and declarative languages is a rather hazy one that we will not attempt to make more specific. In fact, in a qualitative sense it appears difficult to make this distinction at all, since the declarative statement can always be regarded as an imperative statement that builds an entry in a table containing the text of the statement and that is processed subsequently. Furthermore, if we ignore efficiency, there is often a simple translation of a declarative statement into an imperative form. For example,

$$X = Y, \text{ WHERE } P(Y) = Z$$

can be taken to be equivalent to an imperative statement that examines all values exhaustively, looking for a Y that satisfies P(Y) = Z. A good translator will in this case be one that can optimize this exhaustive search, perhaps by knowing the properties of P, or by analyzing the code for P. More significant properties of a translator would thus seem to be the amount that the translator knows of the area about which the program is concerned and the amount of processing that the translator has to do to transform the program into executable code. With this view it is clear that the translator for a declarative language often has more knowledge of a specific area than a general-purpose language translator and also is likely to spend more time in the translation process.

Examples of the use of declarative languages are found in the following areas

1. Calculation of stresses in engineering structures.
2. Logical design of computers.
3. BNF-specified syntax analysers.
4. Simulation.
5. Picture specification and production.

In some cases the output of the translator is a data-structure, as in the stress and picture applications, while in the case of others, such as logical design, syntax analysis, and simulation, the result is a program that can be executed by subsequent steps of the job.

Because the declarative language translator is necessarily a special-purpose translator, there has

Declarative and Extendable Languages 49

been and will be a tendency for many different languages to be developed for the various applications areas. It is therefore important that the notion of an extendable language be itself extended to encompass such languages. The type of processing that we might expect to be required by declarative languages is much more elaborate than that required by imperative languages, and so it seems unlikely that the simpler forms of extension can be much use. Instead it seems necessary to give the user more explicit control over the translation process. Accordingly, a programming system for the translation of declarative languages should have a powerful facility for manipulating programs as data, and the representation of such programs should be chosen to facilitate such manipulations.

A PROPOSED DESIGN

The main conclusion that we wish to draw from the preceding discussion is that there is a considerable amount in common between the requirements for the more powerful extendable-language translator and for the declarative-language translator. Both of them require that the programmer be given access to the translator so that he can tailor the language to his own wishes. In all but the simplest cases this implies that the programmer can get involved in the coding of the translator as well as the coding of his own program. Here we would like to point out some of the advantages that result from a design in which the user's program and the translator are written in the same language and are in fact indistinguishable. That is, we are suggesting a prescription for the design of an extendable-language system with the following properties.

1. The system should consist of a set of utility routines, written in the core language. These will include I/O routines, a translator, and executive routines to read in the user's program, translate it, and execute it.

2. Routines provided by the user as part of his program should be indistinguishable from the system routines and can be used to replace the system routines if required.

3. Similarly, data structures defined by the user should be indistinguishable from those used by the system routines and can be used to replace them.

4. The translator should be as simple as possible, so that its operations can be understood readily. It should be designed in a modular fashion, so that parts of it can be changed without affecting other parts. In particular, it should be driven by tables or lists where appropriate, so that changes to the language can be made by modifying these tables or lists.

5. The intermediate forms used by the translator should be such as to permit convenient manipulation by the user when necessary, such as some sort of standardized tree structure.

This type of design has a number of advantages over the more usual one. First, the distinctions between translation and execution phases are removed, so that the result of executing a command or procedure can be used to modify the translator if necessary and can permit convenient conversational use of the system. Second, since the user has access to the translator as a procedure, he can control its invocation and the processing of its results, rather than having to work around a fixed form of use that may not always be appropriate.

To illustrate the value of these properties we will give below some examples of programming in such a system that we have implemented and that we have now been using for more than a year. This system, BALM, has been described in more detail elsewhere and is given in block diagram form in Figure 1. In its current implementation the core language is tree-structured and is executed directly by an interpreter, with the option of

Declarative and Extendable Languages   51

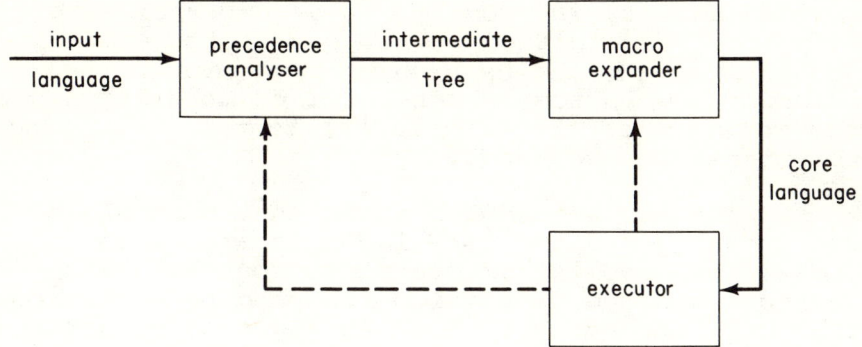

input language   X = A * B + C

core language   (SETQ X (ADD (MPY A B) C))

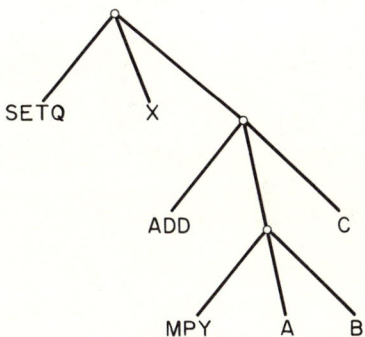

Figure 1

Organization of the BALM System

compiling selected procedures if required. Examples
of the source language and the core language are
also shown in Figure 1. The translator consists of
two phases, an operator precedence analysis phase
driven by lists of operators and a macro-expansion
phase driven by a list of procedures that can be
used to process the intermediate tree.

Extendability is provided in a number of ways ranging from the addition of new operators (which can be done by the novice programmer) through the addition of new macros (which requires more knowledge of the workings of the translator) to the re-writing of the translator routines.

Examples of the command forms in the standard source language and the core language are given in Figure 2, while a list of operators together with precedences and the names of corresponding operations in the core language are given in Figure 3. Macros are associated with the operators =, FOR, WHILE, IF, PROC, EXPR, BEGIN, and the comma. For example, the macro associated with FOR is used to accomplish the transformation shown in Figure 4.

Input Language	Core Language
DO c_1 , c_2 , ..., c_n END	(PROGN c_1 c_2 ... c_n)
BEGIN (v_1, v_2, ...), c_1 , c_2 , ..., c_n END	(PROG (v_1 v_2 ...) c_1 c_2 ... c_n)
GO TO 1	(GO 1)
RETURN e	(RETURN e)
FOR v=(e_1,e_2,e_3) REPEAT c	(FORLOOP v e_1 e_2 e_3 c)
WHILE p REPEAT c	(WHILOOP p c)
PROC(v_1,v_2,...), e END	(QUOTE (LAMBDA(v_1 v_2 ...) e))

Figure 2

Correspondence Between Input and Core Languages

AN EXAMPLE

In this section we will show how a system with the type of facilities described above can be used to provide a very convenient form of extendability. This will permit the user to specify how a new form of expression will be translated by giving its equivalent in the source language. For example, if the user wanted to use the ALGOL 68 form of conditional expression, he could write

   X1 | X2 | X3 MEANS IF X1 THEN X2 ELSE X3;

This will be interpreted to mean that any program whose syntax tree has a subtree T that matches the syntax tree of the expression shown on the left of MEANS, where X1, X2, and X3 are arbitrary subtrees, should be modified by replacing T by the subtree corresponding to the expression shown on the right of MEANS, with the subtrees corresponding to X1, X2, and X3 being replaced by the subtrees that matched them in T. Thus we are able to specify a change in the syntax tree without knowing the details of this tree.

This is implemented in BALM in the following way. MEANS is defined as an infix operator of very low precedence. If the operator | is also defined as an infix operator with appropriate precedence, the above definition will then be translated into the following syntax tree:

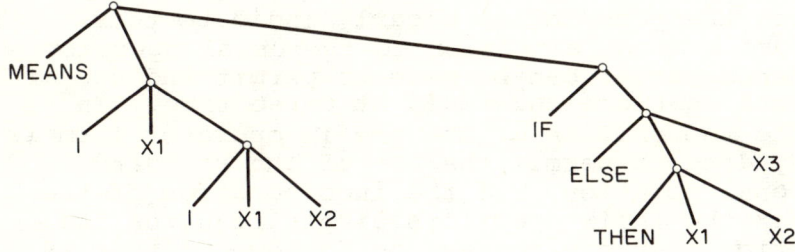

We can then define a macro to be associated with the operator MEANS that can operate on the two subtrees. This macro analyzes the two trees and constructs a macro to be associated with the operator | that can transform any tree that matches the left subtree into the form of the right subtree. To do this we make use of the fact that the macro associated with MEANS can construct procedures that can subsequently be used as macros themselves. The BALM code to implement MEANS is given in the Appendix.

An essential requirement of this method is that the expressions specified in the MEANS definition should be acceptable to the parser. In the case of a simple operator precedence parser this means that the operators should be previously declared. However, in some cases it is possible to deduce which are the operators from the form of the expression. For example, in the following expressions

$$PO \; X1 \quad MEANS \quad ...$$

$$X1 \; IO \; X2 \quad MEANS \quad ...$$

it is apparent that if X1 and X2 are assumed to be operands, then PO is a prefix operator and IO is an infix operator. This can be made more explicit by writing the above as

$$PO \; (X1) \quad MEANS \quad ...$$

$$(X1) \; IO \; (X2) \quad MEANS \quad ...$$

in which the parentheses clearly indicate this. Therefore a minor extension to the usual operator precedence parser can be made to permit the use of operators that are undefined at parse time. In fact the recognition of the prefix operator form is already done to permit the use of the standard functional notation, and the incorporation of the test for the infix operators simply requires the assumption that any operand be followed either by one of a well-defined set of postfix operators or an infix operator. An undefined operator can conveniently be assumed to have high precedence, and will cause a warning message to be issued.

The assignment of precedences can be made more automatic in a number of ways. Algorithms exist for determining precedences from a BNF-language definition if such precedences exist, so new operators can be defined by the addition of new BNF definitions. However, this may require a considerable amount of processing. Alternatively, new operators could be defined by giving examples of expressions with parentheses inserted to indicate how they should be analyzed. Thus the specification

```
        PREC "((X1 | X2) , X3);
```

could declare that | and , were operators and that | has greater precedence than the comma. Combination of this scheme with MEANS could then permit the use of specifications of the form

```
"(FOR((X1=(X2,(X3,X4)))REPEAT X5))
```

```
        MEANS FORLOOP(X1,X2,X3,X4,X5);
```

In the case when the precedences specified were incompatible with previous restrictions, as in the case of the equals sign and the comma in this example, a warning message could be issued, so that the programmer could insert parentheses himself when necessary.

The second essential requirement for the use of the MEANS scheme is that the syntax tree output by the parser have the property that replacement of a variable in an expression by a parenthesized subexpression will give a syntax tree that can be obtained by replacing the variable in the tree by the syntax tree of the subexpression. That is,

$$t(r(v,p,e)) = r(t(v),t(p),t(e))$$

where $t(x)$ is the syntax tree of the expression x, $r(v,y,x)$ is the result of replacing the variable v by y in x, and p is a parenthesized expression. This is clearly true of operator precedence parsers, and in fact of most bottom-up parsers, but is not necessarily true, for example, of a naive top-down BNF-driven parser that inserts all intermediate syntactic levels between an expression and a variable in the syntax tree.

APPENDIX: BALM code for MEANS

```
MMEANS=PROC(L),                              define procedure with argument L
  BEGIN(LS,RS,M,OP,PREVM),                   deifne local variables
  LS = HD TL L, RS = HD TL TL L,             extract operands of MEANS
  M=SUBST(LS,"L",TMAC),                      substitute for L and
  M=SUBST(RS,"R",M),                             R in TMAC
  OP = HD LS,                                extract otp operator
  PREVM = LOOKUP(OP,MACROLIST)               retrieve any previous macro
  IF PREVM=NIL THEN                              and substitute it or
    M = SUBST("ELIS","E,M)                        EXLIS for E in the
  ELSE M = SUBST(PREVM,"E,M),                    modified TMAC
  MACRO(OP,TRANSLATE(M)),                    associate new macro with
  RETURN NIL                                     operator, and return
  END END;

TMAC="(PROC(S),                              define untranslated procedure
  BEGIN(X1,X2,X3,X4,X5,X6),                      to process tree S
  IF MATCH("L,S) THEN                        if tree matches L then
    RETURN BUILD("R)                             rebuild according to R
  ELSE RETURN E(S)                           otherwise process as before
  END END);
```

(continued)

```
MATCH=PROC(L,S),                                    define procedure to match trees
  IF TREEQ(L) THEN
    (IF TREEQ(S) THEN
       (IF MATCH(HD L,HD S) THEN                    return false if trees don't match
          MATCH(TL L,TL S)
        ELSE FALSE)
     ELSE FALSE)
  ELSEIF L "X1 OR L "X2 OR L "X3                    X1 ... X6 are assigned the value
      OR L "X4 OR L "X5 OR L "X6                      of any corresponding
     THEN DO VALUE(L) = S, TRUE END                   subtree
  ELSEIF L S THEN TRUE
  ELSE FALSE
  END;

BUILD=PROC(R),                                      define procedure to rebuild tree
  IF TREEQ(R) THEN
    BUILD(HD R):BUILD(TL R)
  ELSEIF R "X1 OR R "X2 OR R "X3                    replace X1 ... X6 with their
      OR R "X4 OR R "X5 OR R "X6                      current values
     THEN VALUE(R)
  ELSE R
  END;

INFIX("MEANS,O,O,"MEANS):                           define MEANS as infix operator

MACRO("MEANS,MMEANS);                               define macro for MEANS
```

OPERATORS

HD	unary	CAR	2000	
TL	unary	CDR	2000	
$	unary	EVAL	1900	
↑	infix	EXPT	1800	1801
-	unary	NEG	1700	
/	infix	DIV	1601	1600
*	infix	MPY	1601	1600
+	infix	ADD	1501	1500
-	infix	SUB	1501	1500
≡	infix	EQUALQ	1401	1400
GT	infix	GREATERQ	1400	1400
PL	unary	POSQ	1300	
VAR	unary	ATOMQ	1300	
NULL	unary	NULLQ	1200	
¬	unary	NOTQ	1200	
AND	infix	ANDQ	1101	1100
OR	infix	ORQ	1001	1000
→	infix	CONCAT	900	901
:	infix	CONS	800	801
=	infix	SETQ	700	701
REPEAT	infix	REPEAT	600	600
GOTO	unary	GO	500	
FOR	unary	FORLOOP	500	
WHILE	unary	WHILOOP	500	
RETURN	unary	RETURN	500	
THEN	infix	THEN	400	4400
ELSE	infix	ELSE	300	300
ELSEIF	infix	ELSEIF	301	300
IF	unary	IF	200	
,	infix	,	100	101
PROC	bracket	PROC	100	101
EXPR	bracket	EXPR	100	101
BEGIN	bracket	BEGIN	200	
DO	bracket	DO	200	
END	infix	END	1	0
;	infix	;	1	0

Figure 3

Operators, Their Corresponding Procedures, and Their Precedences

FOR I=(J,K,L) REPEAT C

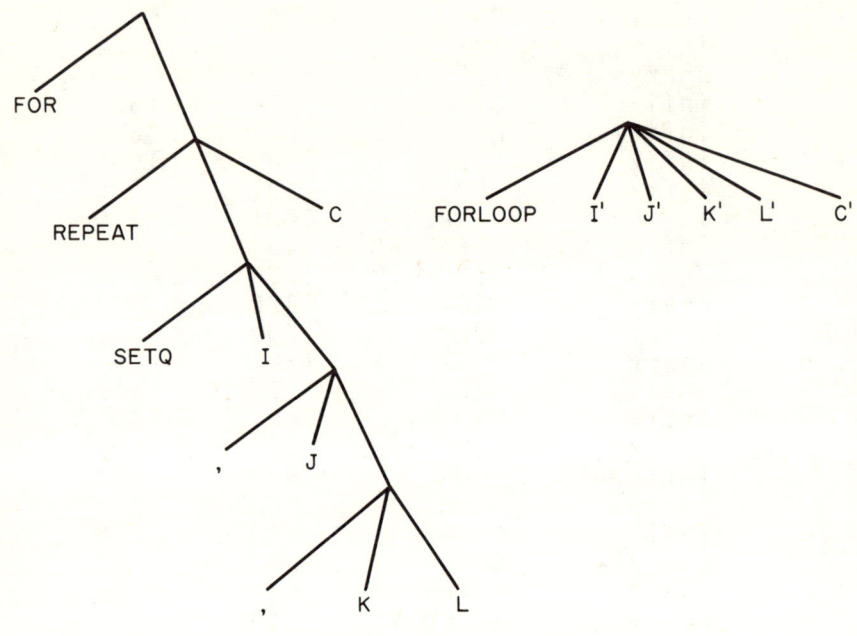

Figure 4

Input Language, Intermediate Tree, and Tree Form of Core Language for a "For Loop"

LOW LEVEL DATA STRUCTURE HANDLING IN A HIGH LEVEL LANGUAGE

Glenn Manacher
Courant Institute of Mathematical Sciences
New York University

A machine-sensitive language inspired by ALGOL 68 and ALGOL W is described. Almost the entirety of the language is machine-independent. The machine-dependent parts are sharply constrained so that the transferral of programs from one machine to another, while not mechanical, is quite straightforward and involves changing a few highly stylized declarations.

Several possible criteria for selecting a language in which to specify an algorithm are represented here today. Jack Schwartz's SETL is perhaps the "purest," in the sense that it gets very close to the essential workings of an algorithm. If one thinks of a program in a conventional language as a mixture of "chaff," which simply maintains data structures, and "wheat," which expresses the essential operation of the algorithm, then undoubtedly SETL programs contain a higher concentration of "wheat" than any other language.

Malcolm Harrison's language, BALM, is also concerned with data structures, but at a sufficiently high level to allow a concise specification of algorithms with a minimum of maintenance overhead. Therefore we may also refer to it as a relatively "pure" language.

By these standards of purity, ESPL, a language I have been designing for the last year, is exeedingly impure. The object of ESPL is to allow a programmar to enjoy two features that might not seem mutually attainable: closeness to the machine on which it is implemented and an abundance of features normally associated with such "high-level" languages as PL/l or ALGOL 68.

The style of an ESPL program is unmistakably "high level," perhaps resembling ALGOL W, its closest relative. It is definitely closer to ALGOL 68 than to PL/360 and yet has most of the machine-level advantages of PL/360 and BCPL.

I have tried to unite the main features of relatively efficient "high-level" and "low-level" languages. What is surprising is that so few of the features actually clash and how easy it is to patch together a compromise when they do.

A high-level language generally has these features:

- Clear, useful syntax
- A variety of *primitive* data structures, such as integers, characters, real numbers, and a binary data
- The ability at the compiler level to specify more complex data structures or *compounds* of primitives, such as arrays, strings, etc., or even compounds of compounds
- Pointers, for address linking and management of data complexes created and organized at run time
- Dynamic allocation of data structures, so that they can be created in arbitrary numbers at run time

Data-Structure Handling 63

- A natural mechanism for allowing some data structures to have an existence limited to an interval within the program's lifetime.
- A declarative mechanism for protecting *types*: no integer operations on real operands, etc. In later versions of ALGOL, such as ALGOL W and ALGOL 68, this has also meant that pointers must be specified at compile time to point to just one class of data structures.
- Perhaps most important of all; maintenance of *control*: By this we mean that the language effectively prevents the execution of code that will result in wild transfers or wild data accesses.

It should be remembered that we are talking here only about high-level languages that purport to be efficient, such as PL/1, ALGOL, etc., and thereby leave out all languages that have as primitive data structures objects that necessarily have a complex internal representation, such as SNOBOL.

The fact that the operations in a high-level language often correspond to common machine operations and that the primitive data structures often correspond to the operands of these machine operations is important, because it is what allows these languages to be implemented with reasonable efficiency. On the other hand, a high-level language will not usually contain with it a machine-level description of the compound data structures, regarding this as an implementation detail. This means that the most naive translation of the user's program — or at least that part that deals with compounds — will be rather inefficient, since he cannot make use of the mapping of the data structure into the computer's memory.

There is a well-known approach to such problems of efficiency: program optimization. The compiler can remove code from loops when it can be performed outside, on entry to the loop; it can attempt to use registers for frequently accessed operands, prevent the performance of operations over constants at run time that could be performed at compile time, substitute constants for variables in loops in which the value of the variable is unchanged, and so forth. To the extent that the optimizer can discover such facts, it can turn poor code into surprisingly good code.

Nevertheless, if a programmer is trying to produce code whose efficiency is close to machine code, dependence on an optimizer is risky. One must know what the optimizer will and will not optimize, and, at the present state of the art, one cannot expect the optimizer to select an optimal representation for a data structure.

For this reason, low-level languages are usually specified in a way that makes them obviously machine-dependent and are understood to correspond in a direct way to the generated code.

In consequence of the limitations of high-level languages (even those equipped with an optimizer) low-level languages attempt to avoid these difficulties by being "conscious," so to speak, of the machine representation of their data structures and operations. The programmer knows about all data structures down to the bit level.

The problems with this approach are also severe: The abstract data structures underlying the algorithm expressed as a program are not referred to concisely; the code, even when heavily documented, does not lend itself to insight into the theoretical framework of the problem; and the code is, of course, not transportable to another machine.

Nevertheless, such languages have been constructed, some of which have a quite pleasing and recursive syntax. BCPL, L6, and PL/360 are examples. In general, these languages adhere to these features:

- Access to some or all of the registers in the machine.

- Data structures set up and maintained at the bit level.
- Large numbers of operations, more or less mimicking the instruction set in the machine.
- Simple conventions for passing parameters to functions.
- Efficient, general, but often "do it yourself" dynamic allocation.
- Address arithmetic on the same arithmetic level as integer arithmetic.
- Absence of a requirement for an optimizer.

A striking feature of most of these languages is that their design shows indifference, if not antagonism, toward the maintenance of control. Closely related is their absence of declarations and, in some cases, block structure. In most cases where these omissions are rationalized, the rationalizations consist of unconvincing arguments about generality, simplicity, and closeness to the machine. The reason these arguments are unconvincing is that the nuclear idea of a low-level language is good enough that it need not be forced to wear a hair shirt of oversimplicity in order to be valuable.

Stripped of the hair shirt and re-outfitted with an ALGOL-style block structure and a mechanism for maintaining control, the criteria for a low-level language may be combined with the criteria for high-level languages, as expressed by the following combined criteria:

- Block structure.
- Clear, useful phrase-structure syntax.
- Data structures and types set up and maintained at the bit level, with the greatest possible dependence on declarations to accomplish this.
- Access to some of the registers in the machines, with a declarative structure that permits the same register to be used for different purposes in distinct blocks and at different recursive levels.
- Pointers, for run-time management of data complexes, with each pointer to a different type

of object itself being a separate type.
- Except for special and known exceptions, no "behind the scenes" data manipulations required by data or programming conventions.
- Obvious deducibility from the source code of what (to a very good approximation) is being done at object level.
- Naive, almost overhead-free, dynamic allocation, linked intimately to block structure, with known data mapping. Control maintained by allocator.
- Protection mechanism just barely sufficient to maintain control.
- Special features, requiring unusual declarations or operators, which permit control overrides where unavoidable.
- Absence of dependence on *global* optimization.
- The order of side-effect propagation left undefined, so that different implementations may achieve greatest efficiency.
- Fastest possible mechanism for entry to and exit from functions and blocks. No inherent block overhead.
- Total absence of interpretive features, except in the debugging aids and input-output.
- In logical expressions, evaluation only of part of expressions necessary to obtain value of the expression.
- Limiting, modifying, or scaling down certain useful high-level features normally associated with high-level languages, when a naive version proves almost as useful and more efficient than the original, *even when* some generality is thereby lost.
- Large operator set, related to instruction set on a typical computer.
- Separate declarations for the *activation* and *scope* of types, variables, and aggregates.
- Low-level analogue to the "union" feature of ALGOL 68.
- Introduction, where necessary, of special *supportive* data structures to permit efficient computation over *standard* ones, where the mapping functions for the standard ones are too complex to permit efficient code without

Data-Structure Handling

the interposition of an optimizer.
- Extensibility.
- Existence of a *nearly transportable subset* of the language whose transportability is restricted only by word length and special registers.

Now let us consider some examples. First, we see a program for adding two complex numbers together. The declaration in the block defines a *bead*, which is a sequence of words in memory in which various *fields* of contiguous bits are defined.

Three variables X, Y, and Z are also defined. These may be in memory (the usual case). However, a limited number of them may be declared to be registers.

```
BEGIN DECL (X,Y,Z) PTR COMPLEX;

    W0 DEF 0,0,32;

        W1 DEF 1,0,32;

            COMPLEX BEAD ((W0,W1) REAL);;
   .
   .
Z = &(W0 = X_W0 + Y_W0, W1 = X_W1 + YW1);
   .
   .
END
```

In the example, a "COMPLEX" is dynamically allocated, and Z is set to point to it. Its W0 field ("real" part) is set to the sum of the real parts of the complexes pointed to by X and Y, and also the W1 field, used to hold the "imaginary" part.

We now consider the first of the almost-as-general features that we substitute in ESPL for the corresponding feature in, say, ALGOL 68. The following is the allocation mechanism.

In ESPL there is both a *stack* for the allocation of data structures local to a *lexical block* (block or procedure) and a *heap* (or *pool*) for dynamic allocation. However, both work somewhat less generally than their correspondents in ALGOL 68. The data structures declared to be *local* must all be set up in the declaration, much like ALGOL 60. However, several "congruent" ones may be set up, and pointers to them may be set up at the same time. In the body of the lexical block, in contrast to ALGOL 68, no more of these may be created, but values of the pointers initially set to each of these "congruent" structures may be freely passed from one to another.

The example just shown allocated "complexes" from the pool. Again, however, the pool mechanism is less general than in ALGOL 68. All data structures allocated via the pool mechanism vanish when the lexical block in which the declaration setting up the class of objects to be allocated — COMPLEX in our case — is exited. The pool thus behaves somewhat like a stack. However, a special provision exists for setting aside locations in the pool to be filled later. This mechanism is initimately coupled to the block structure and provides the ability to permit the allocation of data structure that are *not* next in line to be swept away when a lexical block is exited. The mechanism has the remarkable property that it involves no garbage collection and therefore enables an ESPL program to function in real time despite the presence of a moderately general dynamic allocator, yet it is more general than ALGOL 68's stack mechanism.

The fact that the stack is handled *statically* means that it is possible to implement ESPL so that the amount of overhead on entry to a block is *zero*, unless the block contains some rather fancy declarations. Thus, if a calculation takes place that requires the creation of temporary variables, the act of creating and destroying the variables will typically have no overhead whatsoever.

In our next example, it is desired to create

the data structure shown:

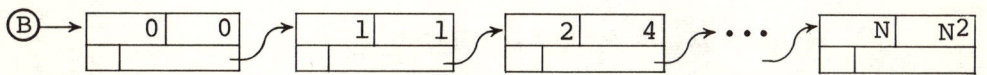

The following program will do it:

BEGIN DECL NODE BEAD ((L0,R0) INTEGER,A1 PTR NODE);

    (B,X) PTR NODE: (N,I) INTEGER::

B = X = &(L0 = 0, R0 = 0);

FOR I INC 1 FROM 1 TO N DO X = X_A1 =

    &(L0 = I, R0 = I*I);
      .
      .
END

    Observe the assignment statement following FOR. This assignment can be any assignment legal in ESPL, so that a FOR statement can be used for chasing down a list by writing FOR X = X_A0 UPTO @0 DO ... .

    One definite defect in our last example is the *default initialization* to "void" implied by the necessary initialization of the A1 field of a NODE on each creation. To get around this, we have a small set of "dangerous" features in ESPL, which *do* compromise ESPLs claim to control-inviolability. These features violate control in the interest of efficiency. In the next example, we see an "improved" version of the last program, which prevents the default initialization of the pointer field and relies on the integrity of the program to ensure control.

B = X = &(L0 = 0,R0 = 0,A1 <u>NOINIT</u>);

   <u>FOR</u> I INC 1 <u>FROM</u> 1 <u>TO</u> N <u>DO</u> X = X_A1 =

      &(L0 = I,R0 = I*I,A1 <u>NOINIT</u>):

         X_A1 = @0;

   ESPL allows one data structure to be written
directly into another, provided that the two have
the same form. This does not mean that they must be
different instances of the same declaration. All
they have to have is the same composition. It
does not matter if their governing declarations
are not in the same lexical block or even if one
is declared to be local while the other is allocated
in the pool.

   Two classes of data structures with the same
composition are called *isomorphs*, and there is a
specific declarative mechanism for setting up an
isomorph. In the next example, we see how this
works.

<u>BEGIN</u> <u>DECL</u> BD <u>BEAD</u> (W0 <u>INT</u>); LIST <u>MV</u> <100>BD;

      X <u>PTR</u> LIST;;
.
.
   <u>BEGIN</u> <u>DECL</u> LIST1 <u>LOCAL</u> LIST <u>PTR</u> (A,B), <u>REF</u> C;;
.
.
         |A| = |C|; |X| = |B|;

   <u>END</u>

<u>END</u>

Data-Structure Handling

In the above example, in the outer block, we have set up a *multiple value* (one-dimensional array) whose components, as always, are beads — in this case, beads of type BD. In the inner block, we have declared a local isomorph of LIST and have created three copies. Two of the copies have pointers to them set up in two local variables A and B. They are, therefore, always addressed indirectly. The third is always addressed directly via a *reference* C, known to the compiler. The vertical bars mean "the data structure that so-and-so points to." Hence |A| means "the data structure that A is currently pointing to."

We mentioned before that ESPL has a penchant for including slightly scaled-down versions of high-level languages, when these appear to suffice for practically every application, but yield lower-level code.

Two more examples of this practice might be mentioned: the ESPL conventions for handling indirect function calls and indirect GOTOs.

In a higher-level language that permits labels to be passed around as function parameters (the intention being to transfer control later to the label passed), the label need merely be somewhere in the program known to the call. The function receiving the label as a parameter has no way to tell exactly where in the program the label came from, since the state of the program is different from place to place and since in particular it is different from one lexical block to another. Since this state must be restored when control is passed to the label, it follows that fairly elaborate information must be passed in with the label in order to allow the program to restore itself to the state appropriate to the label when transferring control to the label.

In ESPL, the need to carry this extra "environmental" information along with the label vanishes if we specify in the declaration

DECL L LABEL IN <name>

where <name> is the name of a lexical block from which the only labels assignable to L must come. This declaration means that the compiler knows the "environment" of L, making it unnecessary for it to be carried along as hidden baggage at run time. The label is represented internally as simply a machine address, nothing more.

The handling of indexes in ESPL is perhaps the most interesting feature. Indexes are a separate data type in ESPL, such as INTEGER or REAL. Consider the following declaration:

BEGIN DECL QQ BEAD ((W0,W1) REAL);

AR ARRAY <8,50> QQ; I INDEX AR <-,#>;

J INDEX AR <#,->; X PTR AR;;

I is declared to be an index which indexes the second dimension, and J is the first dimension of any array of class AR. For instance, to set the W1 field field of the J,Ith element of the array currently pointed to by X to 0, we would write

X<J,I>W1 = 0.0

It is also permissible to use integers in any of the index positions, but an internal conversion will take place that converts them to indixes. The result of this index feature is that internally each index is constrained to have values that are multiples of the distance in memory between adjacent elements of the array. A certain type of "coercion" takes place when a value appearing to be an integer is assigned to an index. For instance, executing "I = 2" does not result in the assignment of the integer "2" to I, but rather two times the "unit" on which the values of I are based. A series of

Data-Structure Handling 73

rules govern this sort of arithmetic.

In addition, the bound checking that normally occurs every time an index is used in an array reference can be suppressed without loss of control. A second and third data type analogous to INDEX, called PARVEX and VEREX (for "partially verified index" and "verified index"), are defined. A PARVEX is checked to make sure it is equal to or greater than its lower bound (always 0 in ESPL) whenever its value is changed; a VEREX checks both bounds. The corresponding bounds are not checked when these objects are used in an array reference.

In the next program, two vectors are added very quickly. Observe that by a simple local optimization, only the upper bound of J needs to be checked in the assignment after FOR. Observe also the curious fact that there is no TO part of the FOR statement; it looks as if the loop will be interminable. There is a subtle rule that states that a failure of the principal operator or principal operand of an assignment statement after FOR will cause the statement to terminate; VEREX violation is such a failure.

BEGIN DECL (X,Y,Z) LOCAL ARRAY<N>Q; Q BEAD (W0 INT);

    J VEREX X;;

    FOR J INC 1 FROM 0 DO X<J>W0 = Y<J>W0 + Z<J>W0;

END

"Contractions" of arrays, similar to cross-sections in PL/1, are defined in ESPL. These are in effect subspaces of the space spanned by an array. ESPL manages to effect the handling of these with no overhead, provided indexes are used. These contractions are in fact pointers to cross sections, adapted in such a way as to be less general than their analogue in PL/1 but exceedingly efficient.

It is in large measure this cross-section feature that enables ESPL to be written in sufficient detail to avoid — or greatly reduce — the necessity of global optimization when dealing with arrays when efficient processing is desired.

Note that it is permissible to write

$$AR \text{ } \underline{ARRAY} \text{ } <N,M> \text{ } BD;$$

observe that the bounds are expressions. This has the effect of declaring that all instances of ARs allocated during execution of the current lexical block will be of size N by M, where it is the values of N and M, evaluated once on entry to the lexical block, that control the sizes of the aggregates. The indexing methods just outlined all work satisfactorily when this convention applies.

An example of the detailed use of these features is seen in the next example, which shows ordinary matrix multiplication: B = C*D, where B, C, and D are pointers to an AR. (The index bound checking is not handled optimally.) The prefix "_" (underline) indicates the generation of a cross-section pointer.

<u>BEGIN</u> <u>DECL</u>(C,B,D) <u>PTR</u> AR; AR <u>ARRAY</u> <20,20>Q;
Q <u>BEAD</u>(W0 <u>INTEGER</u>); (A,Y) <u>CSPTR</u> AR<#,->;
X <u>CSPTR</u> AR<-,#>; Z <u>PTR</u> Q; (I,K1) <u>INDEX</u> AR<#,->;
(J,K2) <u>INDEX</u> AR<-,#>;;
    .
    .
<u>FOR</u> I INC 1 <u>FROM</u> 0 <u>UPTO</u> 20 <u>DO</u> <u>BEGIN</u> A = _C<I,->;
Y = _B<I,->;
<u>FOR</u> J INC 1 <u>FROM</u> 0 <u>UPTO</u> 20 <u>DO</u> <u>BEGIN</u> X = _D<-,J>;
Z = _A<J>;
<u>FOR</u> (K1 INC 1, K2 INC 1) <u>FROM</u>(0,0) <u>UPTO</u>(20,20) <u>DO</u>
Z_W0 INC Y<K2>W0 * X<K1>W0; <u>END</u>; <u>END</u>;
    .
    .
<u>END</u>

Data-Structure Handling 75

A full review of all the other features of ESPL would take too long for this session. I would therefore just like to devote a paragraph or so to a few of them to highlight them.

Arrays have analogues called *flexible arrays* that can vary in size from allocation to allocation. Let X be a pointer to a multiple value whose component beads contain pointers to a *flexible* multiple value.

Consider the statement

X = &(W0 =: & R INC 1) ;

Assume R is an integer initially zero. Here, X is set to point to a multiple value, each of whose W0 fields is set successively to point to freshly created flexible multiple values of increasing size: the first with 1 word, the second with 2, etc. The operator "=:" means "evaluate once for each field." The result is the allocation of a sort of triangular array, as shown in Figure 2.

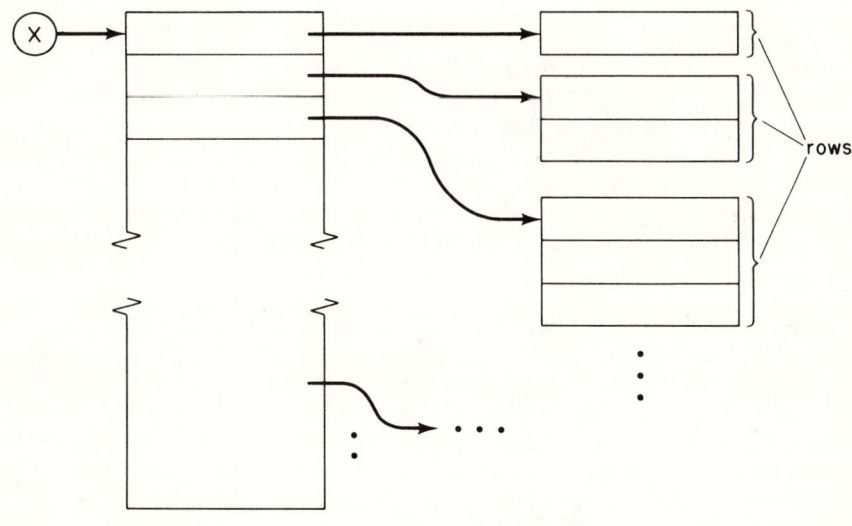

Figure 2

Functions come in recursive, nonrecursive, and system kinds. Function calls have optional *failure exits*, which are labels to which control is passed if the instruction FAIL is executed in the function body.

There are four *storage classes*: allocatable and local, which we have already seen, and two more called *own* and *dummy*. OWN is FORTRAN-like, and DUMMY has no existence of its own, only as a component of a larger data structure. OWN data structures play a special role in making accessible to the program complex tables of data computed at compile time. In addition, they serve as input and output buffers in real-time data processing, whose elements are predefined in ESPL for each real-time implementation.

Debugging features, largely along the lines proposed by Stockton Gaines, are incorporated into the block structure.

Real-time interrupt handling is carefully thought out, and a mechanism is in ESPL for controlling simultaneously various on-line, real-time processes.

Special data structures including strings, special strings with flexible byte width, and several kinds of "hash tables" incorporated into the language. Two kinds of hash tables are distinguished: those in which erasure is possible and those in which it is not. In the latter case, it is permissible to point at a data object stored inside the table.

Input-output is handled at several levels, and a powerful solution is found for the problem of what to do about reading pointers in and out.

Finally, a *macro processor* permits the definition of new statement types in an easy and convenient syntax, and a *code macro* feature permits the identification of new operators with sequences of machine code, which is then embedded into the

Data Structure Handling

generated code by the compiler.

    We now exhibit two final programs. The first is an example of a real-time program designed as follows: Two devices interact with a computer — a rack containing many mouse cages and a clock. Each cage has a bar to be pressed by a mouse whenever a certain stimulus occurs. When this happens, a bufferful of information is transmitted to the computer relating to the condition of the mouse. A "mouse channel" in reality interrupts the computer every time a mouse presses the bar. The computer cannot do all the processing of the data and keep up with the mouse signals, so it stores the inputs for later processing, which begins when an interval clock reaches zero and generates another interrupt. Fifty such runs are to be conducted, each lasting a minute followed by the necessary data processing. A millisecond clock is used. The own bead MOUSE is the input buffer and is so understood by the program.

```
BEGIN DECL LEVELSET (CLOCK,MOUSE);;
FOR I|INT| INC 1 FROM 1 TO 50 DO
   BEGIN DECL MM ALLOC MOUSE;
   BB BEAD(A0 PTR BD, A1 PTR MM);
   X PTR BD;
      IROUTINE MOUSE; X=&(A0=X, A1=&|MOUSE|); ENDI;
      IROUTINE CLOCK; DISGO L2; ENDI;;
   $SETCLOCK(60000); ENABLE; STAY;
   L2:<unravel data from list structure>;
      <publish results>;
   END
END
```

    Here, LEVELSET is a *modal declaration* indicating that the *interrupt routine* servicing MOUSE (the nonrecursive procedure bracketed by IROUTINE and

<u>ENDI</u>) may be interrupted by the CLOCK interrupt but not vice versa. The program works as follows. MM is declared to be an *isomorph* of MOUSE, which is also the name of the buffer into which information is transmitted in connection with the interrupt MOUSE. The MOUSE interrupt routine creates a two-word bead and links it into a growing one-way list. In one of the fields of the two-word bead there is placed a pointer to a newly created MM bead, whose contents are initialized to the current contents of MOUSE. The program remains at <u>STAY</u> while MOUSE interrupts come in; when a CLOCK interrupt comes in, the program transfers control to label L2 without changing the disable/enable state of any interrupt inside the CLOCK interrupt routine. Thus disabled, it proceeds to process the copies of MOUSE accumulated during the run.

Finally, we illustrate how we can use the macro feature of ESPL to provide at least some kind of language extension. We suppose that we have set up a hash table containing strings of some bounded length; this is primitive in ESPL, but time does not permit showing how. Suppose that X is a pointer to such a table. We now wish to enter the word "pumpkin" into the table, with a nice-looking but nonexistent instruction that (we wish) would read

<u>ENTER</u> PUMPKIN,X;

We now set up a *macro definition* — these are embedded in the block structure of ESPL in much the same way as functions — that will "create" this new instruction syntax.

<u>MACRO</u> ENTER(P1, P2 <u>PTR</u> TBL) <u>SPACED</u> ',';
<u>GEN</u>(<u>INSERT</u> ''P1'' <u>INTO</u> P2);
<u>ENDM</u>

INSERT is an ESPL instruction inserting an item into a hash table. SPACED gives the character separating the lexical tokens, in this case, the comma.

   The unusual thing about this macro definition is the presence of information in the second parameter indicating the type of the argument. The notion of type should not by rights exist at macro expansion time; after all, all that is passed in is text. Nevertheless, it is possible with a macro processor integrated into the language — and not merely a preprocessor, as it is in PL/1 — to define types in text arguments in a straightforward and usable way.

   The features described are but a rough sketch of the ESPL design, which is now available through the Courant Institute at New York University ("ESPL: A Low Level Language in the Style of ALGOL").

FLOWCHARTABLE RECURSIVE SPECIFICATIONS

H. R. Strong
IBM Thomas J. Watson Research Center

Recursive definitions of functions in iterative form are known to be easily convertible into flow charts. This paper is concerned with other forms of recursion that are relatively easily and efficiently convertible. Rules for attempting recursive specification of algorithms in these forms and the kind of savings to be achieved by following them are discussed.

The subject of this paper is flowchartable recursive specification, or recursive definitions of functions. The emphasis will be on systematic procedures for obtaining efficient flow-chart-like code from recursion equations and on rules to follow in attempting to make easily flowchartable specifications. The talk will be at a tutorial level: for proofs of some of the claims and elaboration of the details of the algorithms discussed, see [3, 4, and 1].

We will start by discussing recursion removal in a situation in which subroutines (or primitive operations) that we do not want to analyze further are called recursively. Figure 1 illustrates the well-known technique for removing a recursion in iterative form. We could just as well read the branched recursion equation

f(x) = if p(x) then f(a(x)) else if q(x) then b(x).

In terms of the assignment and branching of the flow chart, this is expressed as a decision between p(X) and q(X) (they are assumed to be mutually exclusive; if neither holds, then f(x) is undefined) followed by a loop assigning a(X) to X, in case p(X), and followed by a final assignment of b(X) to F (the location for holding the value of f(x)), in case q(X). The nodes labelled "IN" and "OUT" are assumed to handle I/O operations including an initial assignment of value x to location X.

The branched recursion equation is in *iterative form* because the function letter called recursively appears as the last operation to be performed (on the outside) of the expression in which it occurs. This is what causes the simple loop structure. However, the standard technique used here can be applied almost as easily to branched recursion equations not in iterative form. In Figure 2 the same technique has been applied, but some blanks have been left because we have a *control problem*. The f(b(x)) part of the expression a(f(b(x))) calls for a loop as before. The branch corresponding to q(x) calls for the assignment F → c(X). But the a(f) part of a(f(b(x))) calls for the loop at the bottom of the flowchart with the assignment F → a(F) and we have no way to make the decision for that loop — at least no way explicitly determined by the branched recursion equation.

Now we could fix up a way using only assignment and branching [1]. It would copy the original argument and run through the computation twice: first using only b, and then using a with b as control. But let's make life easy and more reasonable and assume that we have index registers (counters). We use one counter K to count the number of times through the upper loop and then count down to zero as we

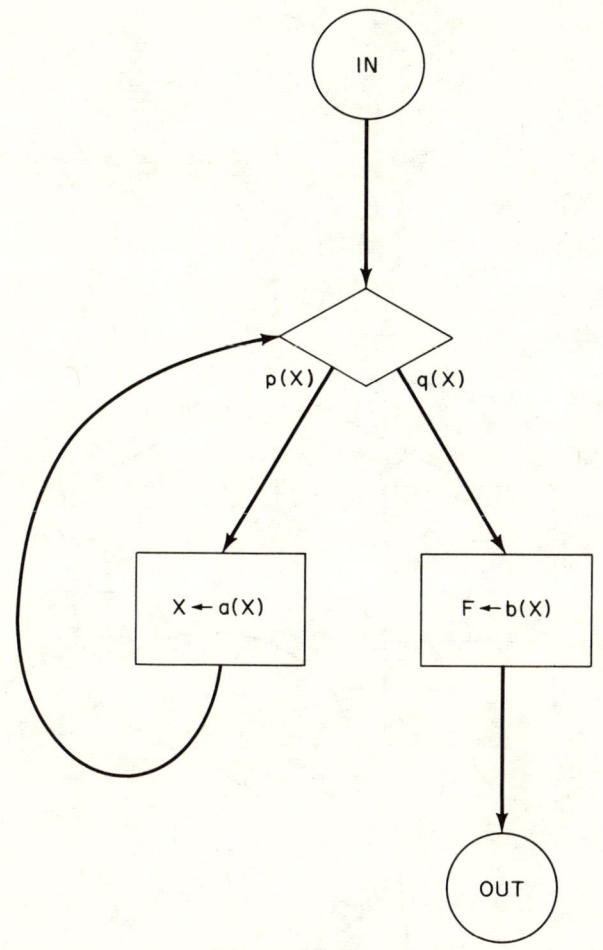

$$f(x) = \begin{cases} f(a(x)) & \text{if } p(x) \\ b(x) & \text{if } q(x) \end{cases}$$

Figure 1

Recursion Removal

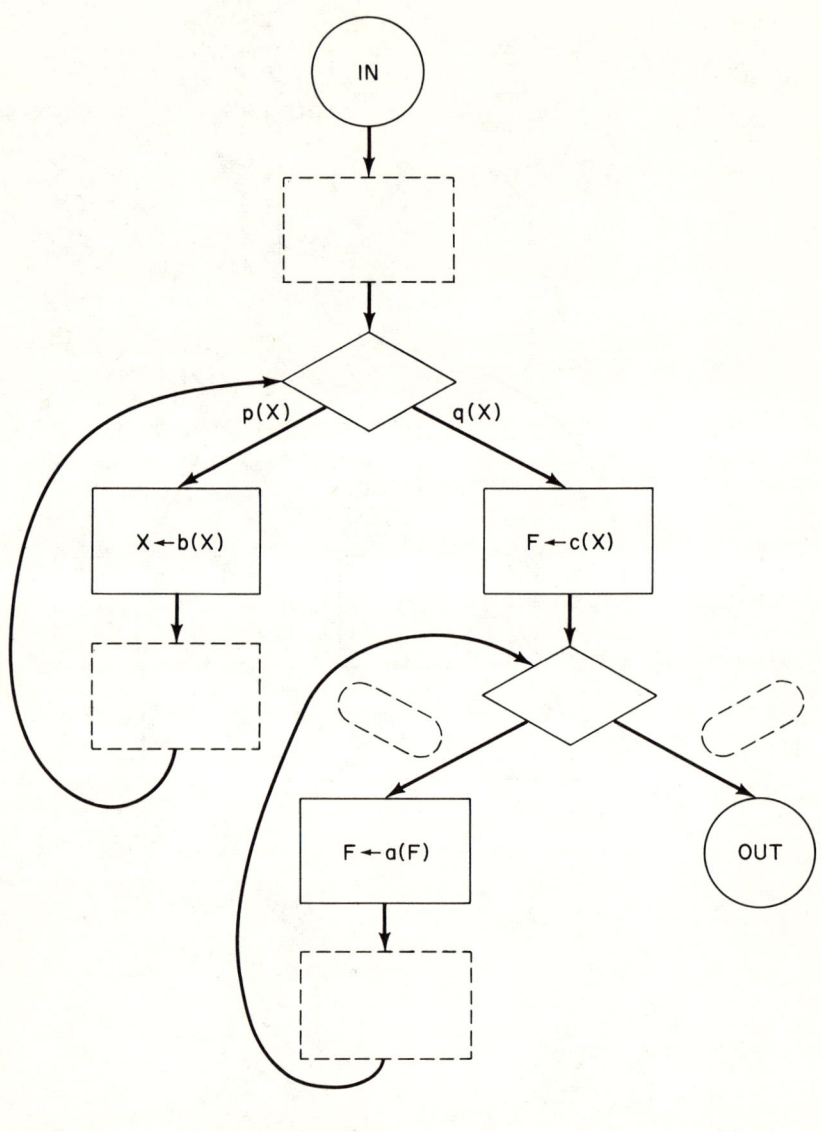

$$f(x) = \begin{cases} a(f(b(x))) & \text{if } p(x) \\ c(x) & \text{if } q(x) \end{cases}$$

Figure 2

iterate the lower loop (Figure 3).

    I want to stress the distinction between the operations on the counter K and the arbitrary and unanalyzed subroutines a, b, c, p, and q and also the distinction between the contents of K (an arbitrary integer) and the contents of locations X and F, which have arbitrary and unanalyzed data structures. Since we have access to unrestricted counters like K we can program them to simulate a pushdown stack *for integers* but not for arguments like x: There is no way to code x into integers because of its arbitrary (unknown) data structure. All we can assume is that the subroutines a, b, c, p, and q access that data structure appropriately. When one of these routines fails to apply to its argument and produce output, then f(x) is undefined.

    Now let's try something more complex, a recursive definition that calls the function defined twice in the same expression (Figure 4). We find the same situation as before except that the two loops are not separated and it is not clear how many times we should go through each. Let's refer to the f being called recursively as a *function letter* and to the other symbols as *operation* and *predicate* symbols. The solution to the control problem is to count something else: the number of function letters left to be executed. At the start there is one function letter to be executed, so the counter K should be initialized to 1. In case p(X) holds, the net effect is an increase of one function letter waiting to be executed, so we set K to K+1. In case q(X) holds, the net effect is a decrease of one, so set K to K-1. Then, if K≠0, the computation is not finished so take the X ← a(F) branch rather than exiting.

    The processes I have described for recursion removal are systematic rather than *ad hoc* and can remove recursions involving arbitrarily many recursive function calls in a single expression. There is no problem with simultaneous or mutual recursion: For each distinct function letter we set up a coroutine (see [3] or [4] for details). But let's

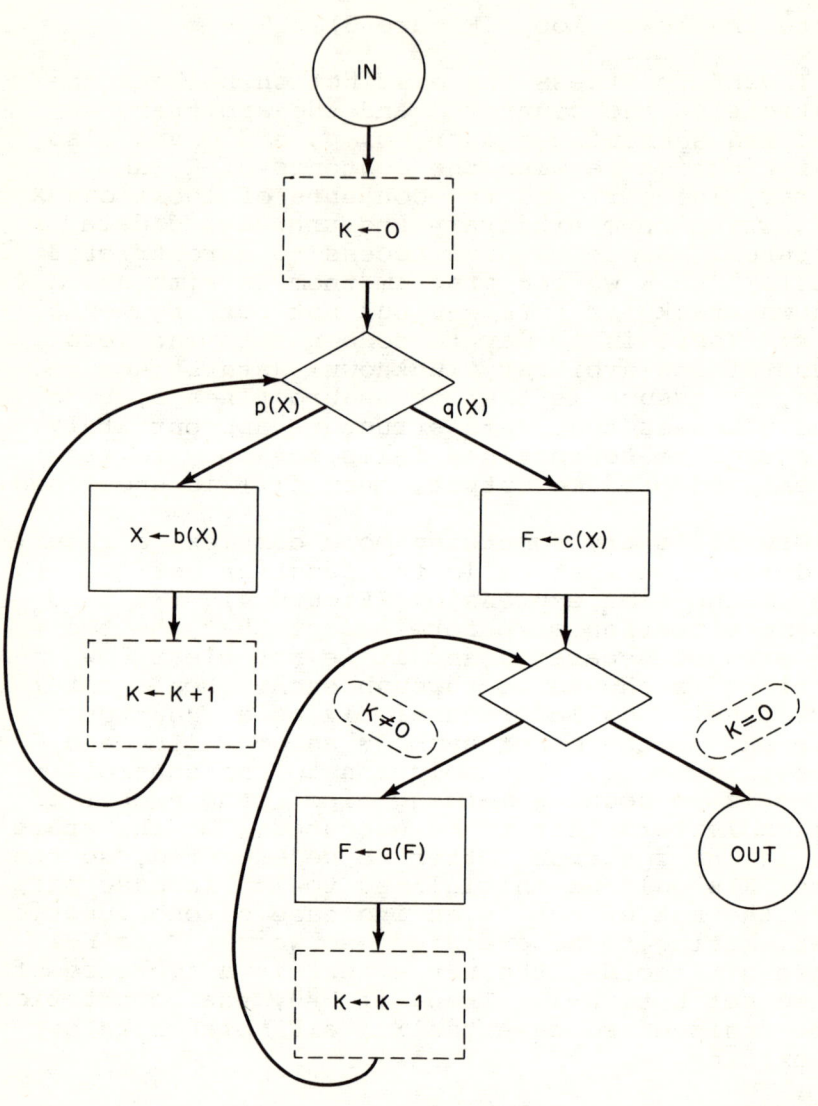

$$f(x) = \begin{cases} a(f(b(x))) & \text{if } p(x) \\ c(x) & \text{if } q(x) \end{cases}$$

Figure 3

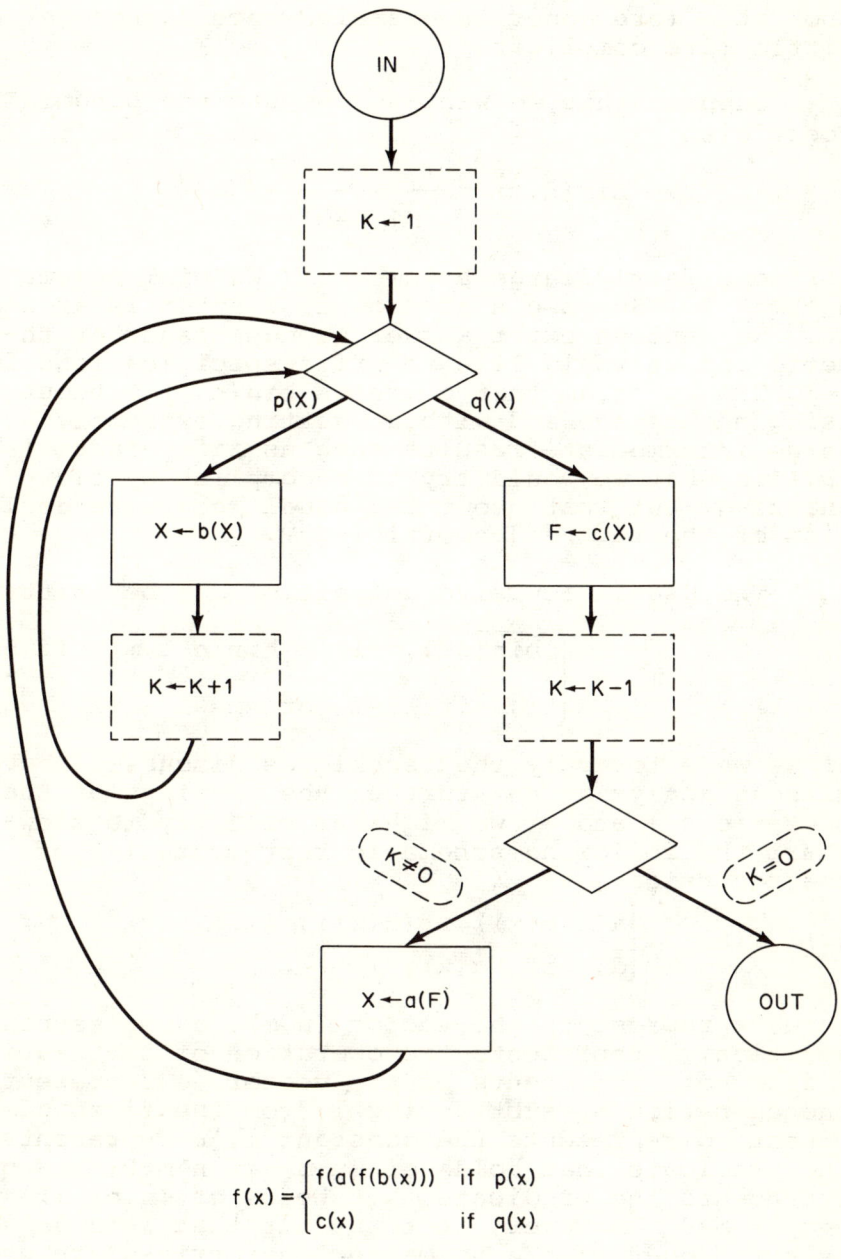

$$f(x) = \begin{cases} f(a(f(b(x)))) & \text{if } p(x) \\ c(x) & \text{if } q(x) \end{cases}$$

Figure 4

look at a more concrete example where things get a little more complicated.

Suppose that we want to compute the binomial coefficient

$$\text{bin}(n,m) = \frac{n!}{m!(n-m)!}$$

for some fairly large arguments. We will assume $n \geq m \geq 0$. Suppose n is around 50 and m is around 10. We want an exact answer using integer arithmetic and we would like to write specifications for a FORTRAN program that computes bin(n,m) without using much space and without getting extremely large intermediate results such as fifty-factorial. This is what we would try to accomplish by flow-charting; but what about the usual recursive definition of the binomial coefficient?

The usual recursive definition can be written

(1) $\quad \text{bin}(n,m) = \begin{cases} \text{bin}(n-1,m-1) + \text{bin}(n-1,m), & \text{if } n>m>0, \\ 1, & \text{if } n=m \text{ or } m=0. \end{cases}$

If we were to apply the techniques discussed above without analyzing any further the meanings of the operations + and -, we might as well try to flowchart the following schematic representative of the recursion:

(2) $\quad f(x) = \begin{cases} a(f(b(x)), f(c(x))), & \text{if } p(x), \\ d, & \text{if } q(x). \end{cases}$

Here, x represents the vector (n,m), a represents addition, b represents the operation of subtracting 1 from both components of the vector, c represents the operation of subtracting 1 from the first component, d represents the constant 1, p represents the predicate that holds of (n,m) if n>m>0, and q represents the predicate that holds of (n,m) if n=m or m=0. However, it turns out that *this schema is not flowchartable* no matter what tricks are used for control. The expressions that arise cannot be

Flowchartable Recursive Specifications   89

uniformly executed with a finite number of locations. This result was first presented at the Second ACM Symposium on Theory of Computing, and a detailed proof appears in [3]. It was also obtained independently by Paterson and Hewitt [1]. The problem is indicated in the way one might attempt to use the recursive definition by setting up an array with "dimension" the size of the largest expected argument and line-by-line computing all the binomial coefficients up to the one desired. Unless one wants all the binomial coefficients, this will be extremely wasteful in terms of time and space, and the dimension declaration will have to depend on the input arguments.

This problem suggests a first rule for constructing easily flowchartable recursive specifications. We say that an expression has *nested* function letters if the positions at which function letters occur are always comparable with respect to the tree ordering. Otherwise (i.e., if there are occurrences of function letters that are incomparable with respect to the tree ordering) the expression is said to have *unnested* function letters. Thus f(a(f(b(x)))) has nested function letters, while a(f(b(x)), f(c)x))) has unnested function letters.

RULE I: ALWAYS CHOOSE EXPRESSIONS WITH
         NESTED FUNCTION LETTERS

If it is impossible to follow Rule I, then it is probably impossible to get efficient flow-chart code without calling for some facility for pushdown storage. It happens that, in the case of the binomial coefficient, we do have an alternative to (1) that involves only nested function letters:

(3) $bin(n,m) = \begin{cases} \frac{n}{m} bin(n-1,m-1), & \text{if } n > m > 0, \\ 1, & \text{if } n = m \text{ or } m = 0; \end{cases}$

or, as a schema,

(4) $f(x) = \begin{cases} a(x, f(b(b))), & \text{if } p(x), \\ d, & \text{if } q(x). \end{cases}$

In (4) a represents an operation with (effectively) three integer arguments (since x represents (n,m) that computes the product of the first and third divided by the second. For reasons that will become clear later, we note that this operation can be computed in integer arithmetic, so that, when the result is an integer, the intermediate results of the computation are bounded in size by the maximum of the arguments or the result.

In the application of recursion removal techniques to (4) another problem arises because the argument x occurs outside the scope of the function letter f. This is no problem in principle. Patterson and Hewitt have shown that any such recursion can be removed using only assignment and branching (not even counters), but the chart produced is extremely complex and inefficient [1]. This problem suggests

RULE II: TRY TO KEEP ARGUMENTS INSIDE THE
SCOPE OF ALL FUNCTION LETTERS

Of course, if the function letters were unnested, Rule II could not be followed.

Figure 5 illustrates the difficulty of applying the recursion removal techniques discussed above to (4). There is no real control problem: A counter can take care of control, as in Figure 3. The problem is one of storage: Where can we get the left argument for the assignment F ← a(, F) in the lower loop? The value in X at the finish of the upper loop is not the appropriate argument for the first time through the lower loop but b of it. Similarly, it is b of b of the argument appropriate for the second iteration of the lower loop, etc. This situation suggests a possible solution. Suppose b is invertible. It need only be invertible for the arguments to which it was applied in the upper loop. Thus suppose we have an operation e such that e(b(x)) = x if p(x). Then we can fill in the flow

Flowchartable Recursive Specifications

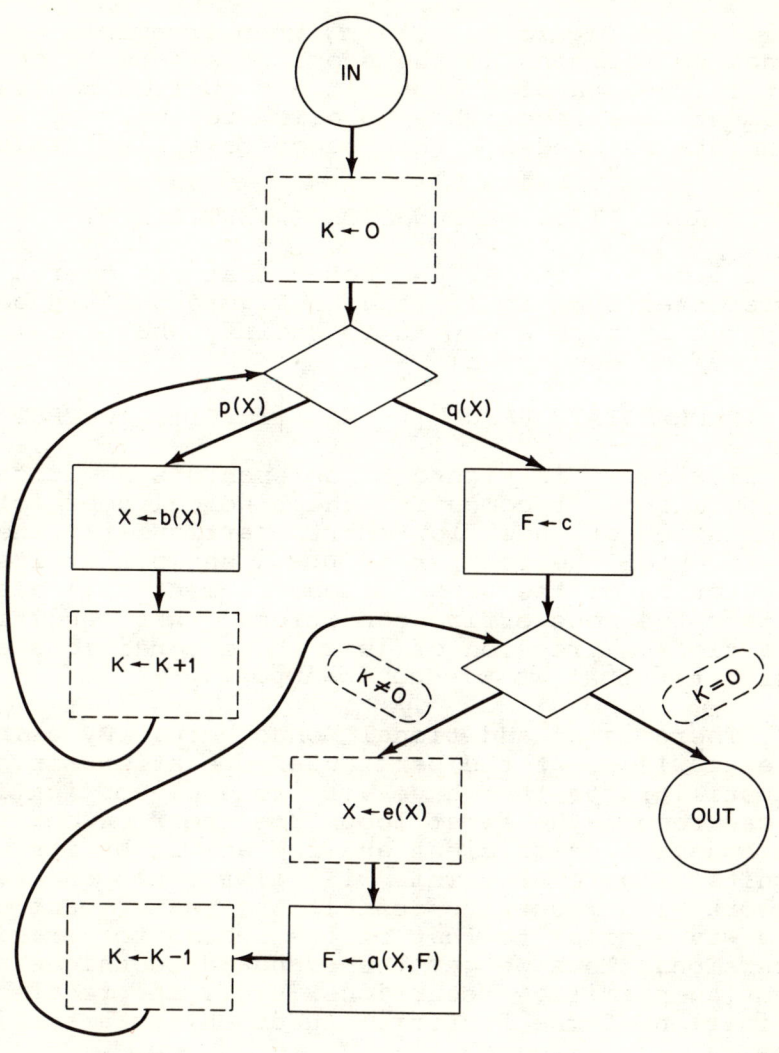

$$f(x) = \begin{cases} a(x, f(b(x))) & \text{if } p(x) \\ c & \text{if } q(x) \end{cases}$$

ASSUME b INVERTIBLE:
$e(b(x)) = x$ if $p(x)$

Figure 5

chart as in Figure 5. Often, when arguments
cannot be kept inside the scope of all function
letters, enough of the operations applied to the
arguments are invertible to allow recovery of the
arguments as needed. This suggests a final rule:

RULE III: MAKE USE OF INVERTIBILITY

Why follow the rules? We noted that the operation
represented by a in (4) and in Figure 5 could be
computed in such a way as to satisfy what I call a
nonoverflow condition:

$|\text{INTERMEDIATE RESULT}| \leq \text{MAX}\{|\text{INPUT}|, |\text{OUTPUT}|\}$

The flow chart in Figure 5 represents schematically
a flow chart for computing the binomial coefficient.
Examination of this flow chart, particularly the
way in which the counter is used, shows that its
computation of the binomial coefficient will also
satisfy the nonoverflow condition. This condition
is a tight expression of just those conditions of
efficiency that we wished to impose.

There is an additional bonus here. By using
more knowledge of the particular operations involved
but still facts that have very general application,
we can remove the first loop from the flow chart for
the binomial coefficient and replace it by its
results (Figure 6). This will always happen when
we work with recursive definitions that "count down"
in a way similar to that of the schema for primitive
recursion. Thus we get the standard technique for
removing primitive recursions (e.g., the recursive
definition of the factorial function) as a special
case.

Now I have given illustrations of the cases in
which the techniques work well. The examples might
indicate that if enough operations are invertible
and if the function letters are nested, then the
recursion can easily be removed. However, there is
a point at which we have to stop using the counters
as counters and use them to record a bit string.
In Figure 7 the problem with following the techniques

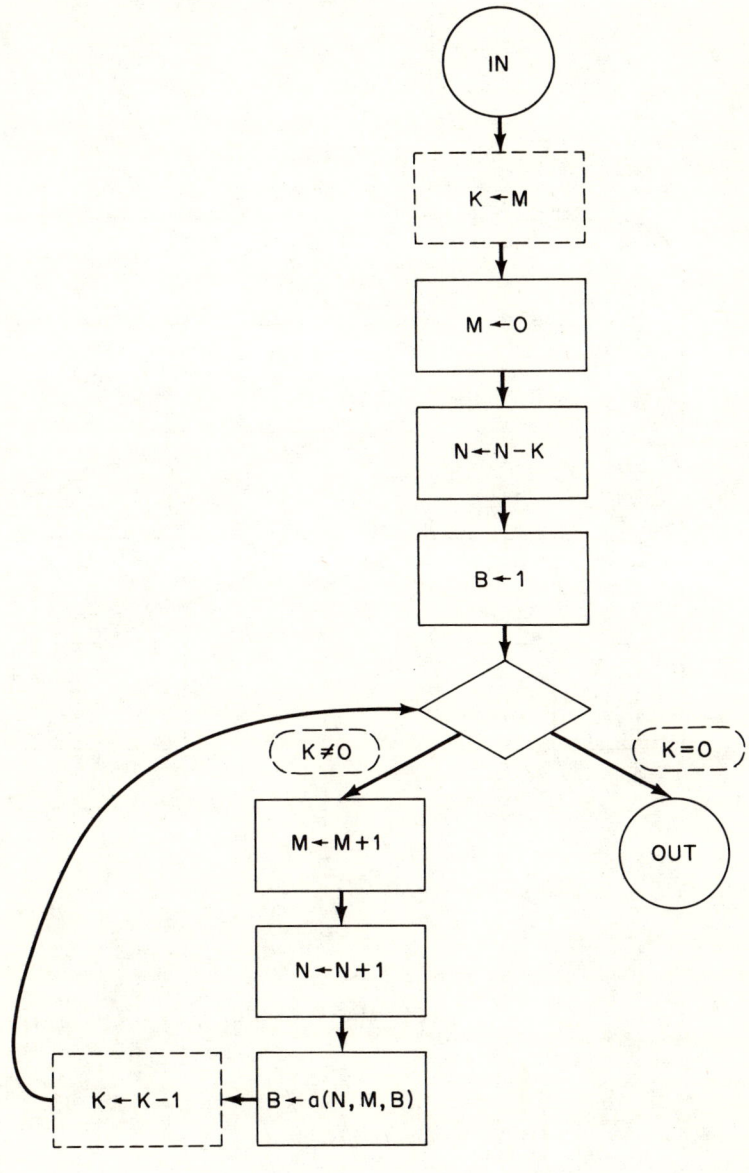

THE FIRST LOOP CAN BE REMOVED:

Figure 6

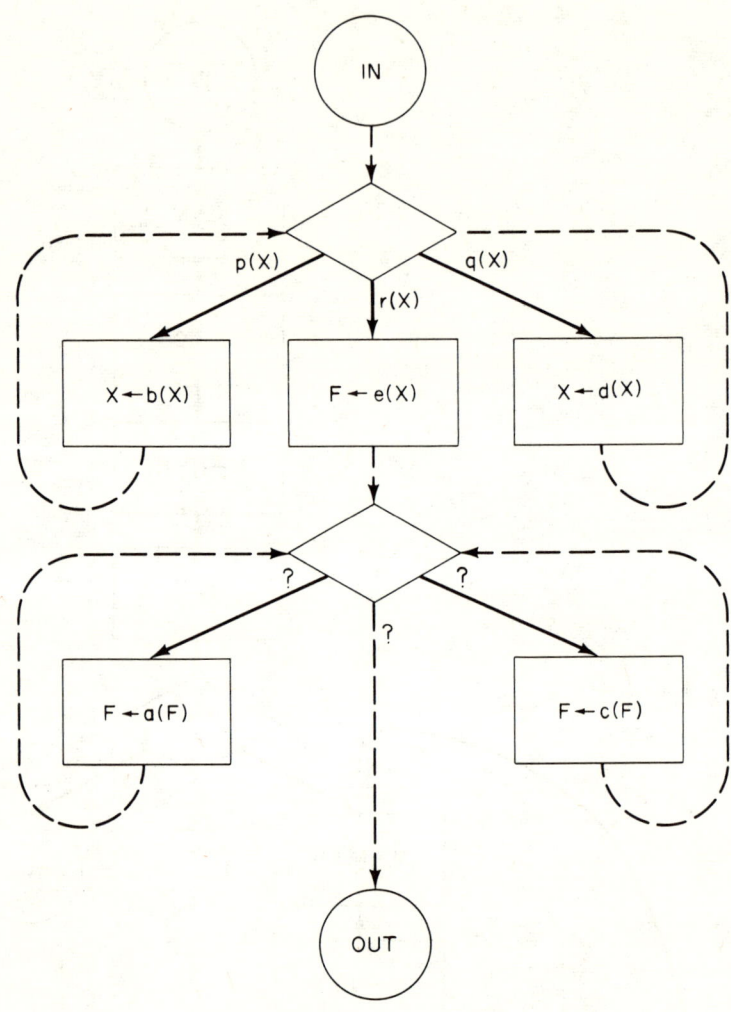

TOO MANY CHOICES

$$f(x) = \begin{cases} a(f(b(x))) & \text{if } p(x) \\ c(f(d(x))) & \text{if } q(x) \\ e(x) & \text{if } r(x) \end{cases}$$

Figure 7

described above is one of control. We will want to take the lower left loop once for each time we take the upper left loop and behave similarly for the right loops. But order is important. It may be that, for each x, at most one of $(\exists y)[p(y)$ & $b(y) = x]$ and $(\exists y)[q(y)$ & $d(y) = x]$ can hold, so that sufficient invertibility will allow a solution of the control problem. However, this solution is likely to be extremely expensive in time, with many retestings of the same arguments. In order to follow the simple flow of Figure 7 without these special invertibilities, a bit string describing the path through the upper loops must be recorded. In this situation we are forced to sacrifice either a nonoverflow condition — letting counters grow exponentially — or time efficiency. Loosely speaking, there is no middle ground between restricting the counters to grow linearly (being used to count iterations of loops) and letting the counters grow exponentially. If a recursion can be removed in the straightforward way of the earlier examples, then it can be done using a single counter (for each recursion removed) — a single counter that grows only linearly with the number of noncounter instructions executed. The question of when restricted counter control can be added to a flow chart, generated by the straightforward generalization of the technique for removing iterative form recursions, is decidable. The decision procedure amounts to trying the technique and seeing if too many choices are produced [4].

Suppose we call the object represented by one of the schemata above a *functional* and treat it as a function of its subroutines (operations and predicates) as well as its arguments. We know not all recursive functionals are flowchartable in contrast to the fact that all partial recursive functions are flowchartable. There is no known syntactic characterization of the flowchartable recursive functionals; but the only way recursive functionals have been shown to fail to be flowchartable is through unnested function letters.

REFERENCES

[1] Patterson, M.S., and C.E. Hewitt, "Comparative Schematology," *Record of the Project MAC Conference on Concurrent Systems and Parallel Computation*, Woods Hole, Massachusetts, 1970, ACM 1970.

[2] Strong, H.R., "Translating Recursion Equations into Flow Charts," (Extended Abstract), *Conference Record of Second Annual ACM Symposium on Theory of Computing*, Northampton, Massachusetts, 1970, ACM 1970.

[3] ———, "Translating Recursion Equations into Flow Charts," To be published in the *JCSS*, 1971.

[4] ———, "Removal of Simple Nonlinear Recursions Without Pushdown Stores and Removal of Simple Linear Recursions," *IBM Technical Disclosure Bulletin*, 13:5, 1970.

THE EXPRESSION OF ALGORITHMS BY CHARTS

John Bruno
Kenneth Steiglitz
Princeton University

The purpose of this paper is to discuss the expression of algorithms by flow charts and, in particular, by flow charts without explicit go-to's (D-charts). For this purpose, we introduce a machine-independent definition of algorithm that is broader than usual. Our conclusion is that D-charts are in one technical sense more restrictive than general flow charts, but not if one allows the introduction of additional variables that represent a history of control flow (flags). The use of these flags can encourage us to exhibit clearly rules for determining flow of control, and it is in this sense that D-charts can be considered good means for expressing and communicating algorithms.

INTRODUCTION

The term "algorithm" is used in many different ways. Sometimes we speak of an algorithm as a process in the abstract, without reference to a particular computer. It is in this sense, for example, that we speak of the "radix exchange sort algorithm," or the "simplex algorithm." Often we identify an algorithm with a particular sequence of instructions for a particular computer.

In this paper we shall present a new definition of algorithm that emphasizes the sequence of commands associated with a particular "input." We then define the notion "expression" of algorithms by general flow charts and flow charts without explicit go-to's (D-charts). Some theorems are given that exhibit some of the relationships among algorithms, flow charts, and D-charts.

ALGORITHMS

Central to our discussion is the notion of an algorithm, which is defined independently of its expression in a given language. One such definition of an algorithm can be given as follows:

Let N be a set of *variables* or *names*. If $n \epsilon N$, then n takes on *values* in a *value set* V_n. Let C be a finite set of "sufficiently basic" operations called *commands*. All members of C are of the form

$$y \leftarrow f(y_1, \ldots, y_k), \text{ where } k \geq 0, y_1, \ldots, y_k$$

are members of N and f is some function of the values of the names $y_1, \ldots, y_k$. A function s which associates with each member of N a value in the corresponding value set is called a *state function*; that is, if for every $n \epsilon N$, $s(n) \epsilon V_n$, then s is called a state function. Let S denote a prechosen class of state functions called *initial state functions*. An *algorithm* A is a function which associates with each member $s \epsilon S$ a finite sequence A(s) of members of C (possibly the null sequence λ). *The execution of A with respect to $s \epsilon S$ is a finite sequence $s_0 s_1 \ldots s_u$ of state functions determined by:*

1. $s_0 = s$.
2. Suppose $y \leftarrow f(y_1, \ldots, y_k)$ is the ith term in the sequence A(s), then

Expression of Algorithms by Charts

$s_i(n) = s_{i-1}(n)$ for all $n \in (N = \{y\})$
and $s_i(y) = f(s_{i-1}(y_1), \ldots, s_{i-1}(y_k))$.

3. u is equal to the number of terms in $A(s)$.

Example 1: Algorithm FACTORIAL

$N = \{M, MF, K\}$, where the values of M, MF and K are integers, and $C = \{c_1, c_2, c_3, c_4\}$, where $c_1 \triangleq MF \leftarrow 1$, $c_2 \triangleq K \leftarrow 1$, $c_3 \triangleq K \leftarrow K+1$, $c_4 \triangleq MF \leftarrow MF \cdot K$. The initial state functions must assign a nonnegative value to M, therefore $S = \{s \mid s \text{ is a state function and } s(M) \geq 0\}$. If $s \in S$, then

$$\text{FACTORIAL}(s) = \begin{cases} c_1 & , s(M) = 0 \text{ or } 1, \text{ and} \\ c_1 c_2 (c_3 c_4)^{s(M)-1} & , s(M) \geq 2; \end{cases}$$

where $(c_3 c_4)^k$ means $c_3 c_4 \equiv (c_3 c_4)^1$ concatenated with $(c_3 c_4)^{k-1}$ [$(c_3 c_4)^0 = \lambda$]. Informally, this algorithm sets MF equal to M factorial.

Example 2: Algorithm SEARCH

$N = \{M, \text{list}[\,], \text{count}[\,], i, x\}$. We are using list, list[ ], and count[ ] to denote a countably infinite number of names; specifically, list[ ] is shorthand for the names list[1], list[2], ..., list[M]. $S = \{s \mid s(M) \geq 1\}$.

Informally, this algorithm searches list[1], ..., list[M] for x. If it is found at position j, say, count[j] is incremented by 1. If it is not found, it is appended to the list at position M+1, count[M+1] is initialized at 1, and finally M is incremented by 1.

Let $C = \{c_1, \ldots, c_6\}$

$$c_1 \triangleq i \leftarrow 1$$
$$c_2 \triangleq i \leftarrow i + 1$$
$$c_3 \triangleq \text{count}[i] \leftarrow \text{count}[i] + 1$$
$$c_4 \triangleq \text{list}[i] \leftarrow x$$
$$c_5 \triangleq \text{count}[i] \leftarrow 1$$
$$c_6 \triangleq M \leftarrow i$$

SEARCH is given formally by

$$\text{SEARCH}(s) = \begin{cases} c_1(c_2)^{j-1} c_3 & \text{if } s(x) = s(\text{list}[j]) \\ & (1 \leq j \leq s(M),\ j\ \text{small}) \\ c_1(c_2)^{s(M)} c_4 c_5 c_6 & \text{if } s(x) \neq s(\text{list}[j]) \end{cases}$$

The above definition of an algorithm employs only the sequence of commands to be carried out and says nothing about how one determines the appropriate command sequence for each initial state function. This allows us to discuss the idea of having more than one expression for a given algorithm. Our primary concern is with the finite expression of algorithms by charts that indicate in a schematic way the "flow of control" from command to command.

FLOW CHARTS AND D-CHARTS

Clearly, if there are only a finite number of allowable initial state functions, one could simply catalogue the appropriate command sequences of an algorithm. Complications arise when there is an infinite number of possible initial state functions. We shall use a special class of flow charts called D-charts as a means of expressing algorithms.

By a *flow chart* F we mean a finite directed graph that satisfies the following:

1. Each of the vertices of F must be one of the following types:

   a) Start vertex:

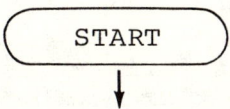

F contains precisely one start vertex and this vertex has exactly one edge incident away from it and no edges incident toward it.

   b) Stop vertex:

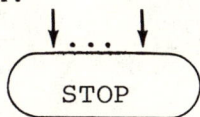

F contains precisely one stop vertex and this vertex has one or more edges incident toward it and no edges incident away from it.

   c) Command type:

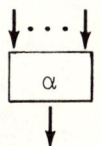

α is a sequence of commands; there are one or more edges incident toward a command vertex; exactly one edge is incident away.

   d) Decision type:

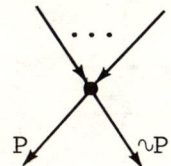

There are two edges leaving a decision vertex; one of these edges is labeled with a *quantifier free* predicate P and the other with $\sim$P, the negation of P; there are one or more edges incident toward a decision vertex.

2. F is a connected graph (in the undirected sense).

We consider a quantifier-free predicate to consist of "atoms" that are combined according to the rules of the propositional calculus. The atoms are relations of the form $R(y_1,...,y_k)$ where $y_i \in N$ for $i = 1, ..., k$, $k > 0$; R takes on the value "true" or "false" when we substitute the values of the variables y_i in $R(y_1,...,y_k)$.

D-Charts (after Dijkstra [1]) are a restricted class of flow charts defined recursively by the following grammar:

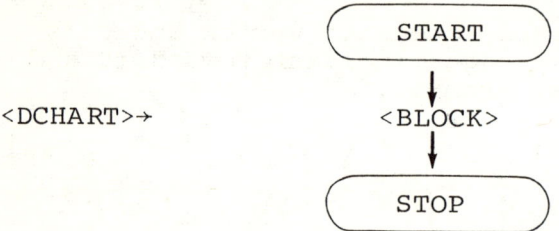

<BLOCK>→<COMMAND> | <ENUMERATION> | <ITERATION> | <BLOCK>
                                                              ↓
                                                          <BLOCK>

<COMMAND>→ [α]   (α is a sequence of commands)

Expression of Algorithms by Charts   103

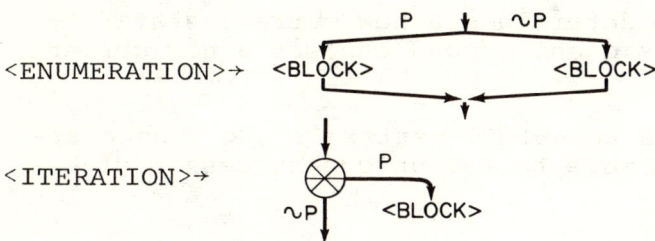

Note that the following conventions have been used:

1. In the ENUMERATION rule we have used

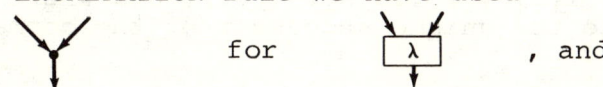

2. In the ITERATION rule we have used

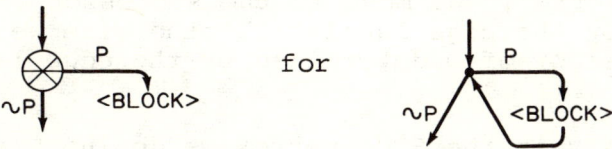

It should be clear that this last convention causes no difficulty in determining where to return after we have "executed" <BLOCK>.

The quantities defined for algorithms in the previous section are defined analogously for flow charts; thus we may speak of the set N of variables of a flow chart F, the set S of initial state functions of F, and the set C of commands associated with F. The sequence of commands and state functions associated with each $s \varepsilon S$ is determined by F as follows: Initially, we have $s \varepsilon S$ as our current state function, a command sequence c equal to λ, a state function sequence $\sigma = s$, and we are positioned at the START vertex of F.

Suppose we are at a vertex $\nu \varepsilon F$, with the current state function s', current command sequence c, and current state function sequence σ. We shall describe how one determines a new current state function, updates c and σ, and chooses a new current vertex in F:

(1) If ν is the START vertex, s', c, and σ are unchanged and we move to the unique successor of the START vertex.

(2) If ν is a command vertex and $\alpha = c_1 c_2 \ldots c_m$, then c becomes $cc_1 c_2 \ldots c_m$, s' becomes s_m, and σ becomes $\sigma s_1 \ldots s_m$; where if $c_i \equiv y \leftarrow f(y_1, \ldots, y_k)$, then $s_i(n) = s_{i-1}(n)$ for all $n \in N - \{y\}$ and $s_i(y) = f(s_{i-1}(y_1), \ldots, s_{i-1}(y_k))$, and where $s_0 = s'$. We move to the unique successor of the command vertex.

(3) If ν is a decision vertex, s', c, and σ remain unchanged. We evaluate P with respect to s', and if P is "true," we move to the successor of ν determined by the edge labeled P, otherwise we move to the successor of ν determined by the edge labeled $\sim$P.

(4) If ν is the STOP vertex we define F(s)=c and define the *execution of F with respect to s* to be σ.

Let F be a flow chart and let N', V'_n for each $n \in N'$, C' and S' be associated with F. Let A be an algorithm and the quantities N, V_n for each $n \in N$, C and S be associated with A. We say that F *directly expresses* algorithm A if:

1. $N = N'$, $V_n = V'_n$ for each $n \in N$, $C = C'$, $S = S'$, and

2. For each $s \in S$, $F(s) = A(s)$.

Let $\xi_d(A)$ denote the set of flow charts which directly expresses algorithm A.

Direct expression of an algorithm does not always provide easily understood flow charts, and accordingly we say that F expresses algorithm A if

Expression of Algorithms by Charts

1. $N \subseteq N'$, $V_n = V'_n$ for $n \varepsilon N$, $c \subseteq C'$, $S = S'/N$ (S'/N denotes the set of functions obtained by restricting the members of S' to the set N), and

2. For each $s \varepsilon S$, $A(s)$ is a subsequence of $F(s')$, where s' is any member of S' whose restriction to N is equal to s, and the state functions in the execution of A with respect to s are equal to the restrictions to N of the corresponding state functions in the execution of F with respect to s'.

Let $\xi(A)$ denote the set of flow charts that expresses algorithm A. Since flow charts are necessarily finite, it may be that $\xi(A) = \emptyset$. Furthermore, $\xi_d(A) \subseteq \xi(A)$.

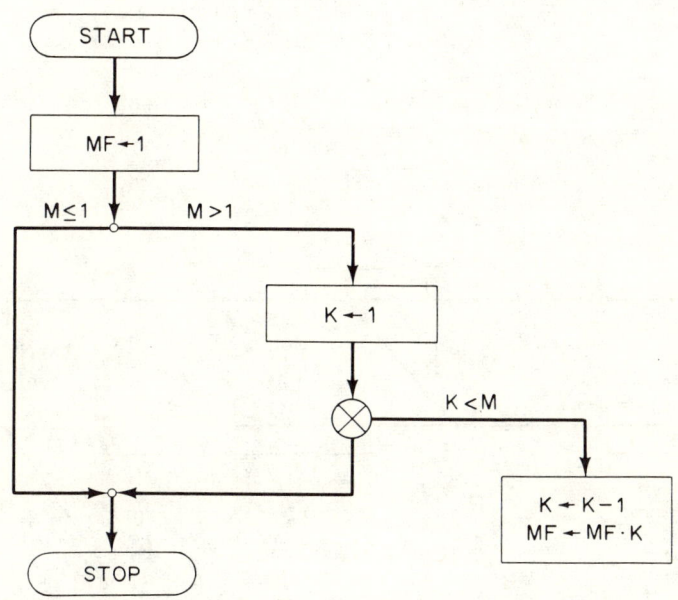

A D-Chart Which Directly Expresses
Algorithm FACTORIAL

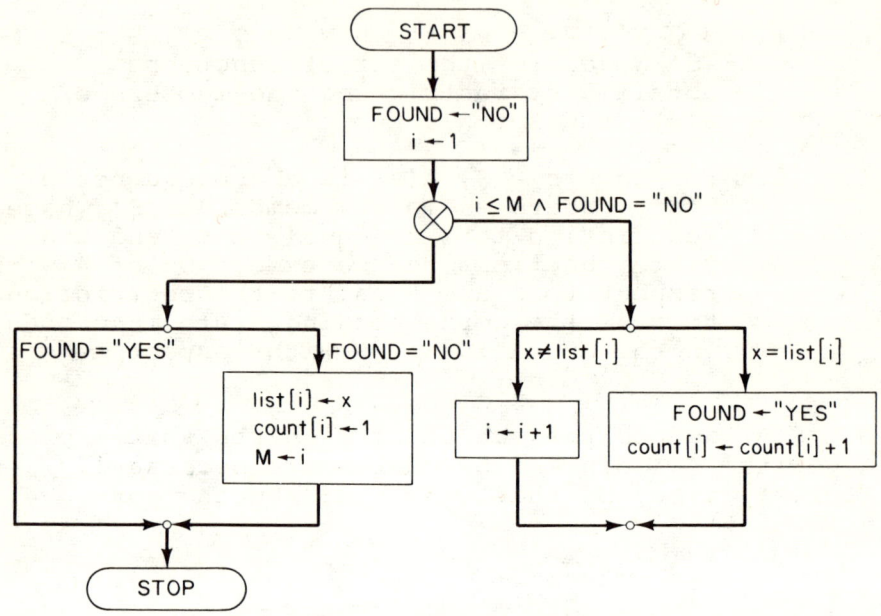

A D-Chart Which Expresses
Algorithm SEARCH

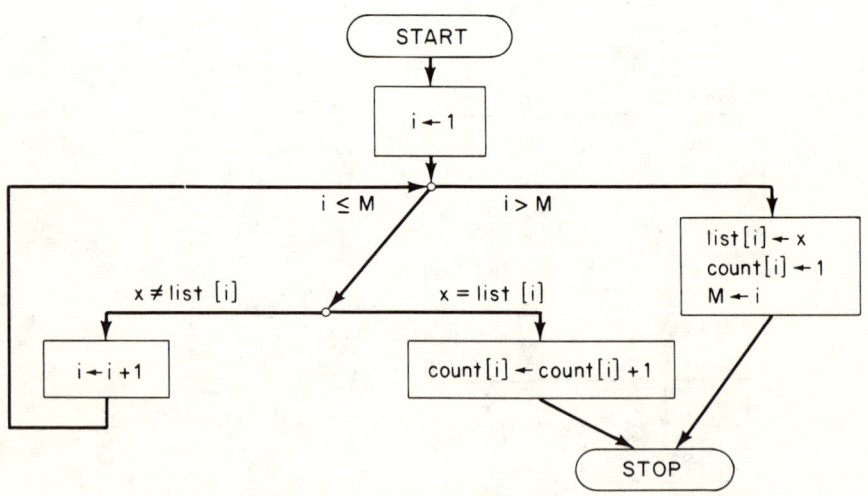

A Flow Chart Which Directly Expresses
Algorithm SEARCH

Expression of Algorithms by Charts

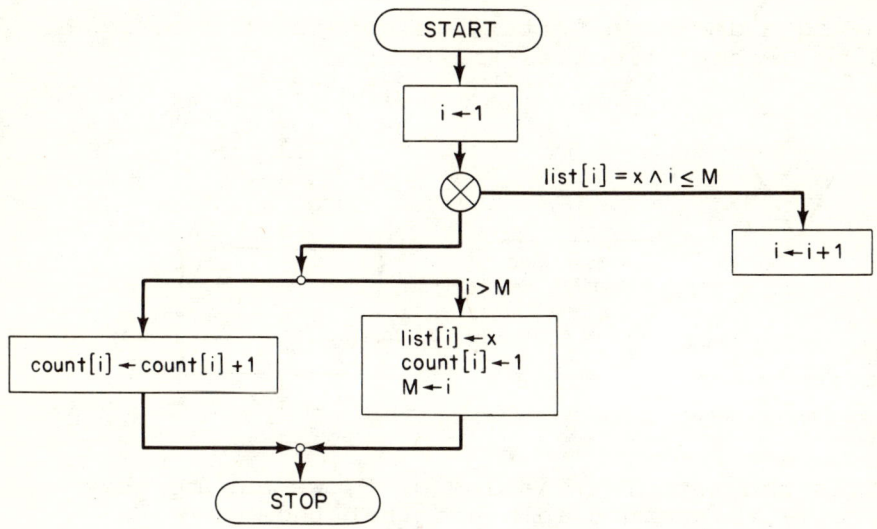

A D-Chart Which Directly Expresses Algorithm SEARCH

D-Charts are as "powerful" as flow charts in the following sense:

Theorem 1: (Bohm and Jacopini [3]) If $F\varepsilon\xi(A)$ then there exists a D-chart $D\varepsilon\xi(A)$.

Proof: Label the START vertex in F with n_0 and the STOP vertex with n_∞ and label all other vertices of F with the labels $n_1,\ldots,n_m$. If n_i is a command vertex we construct a corresponding D-chart block as follows:

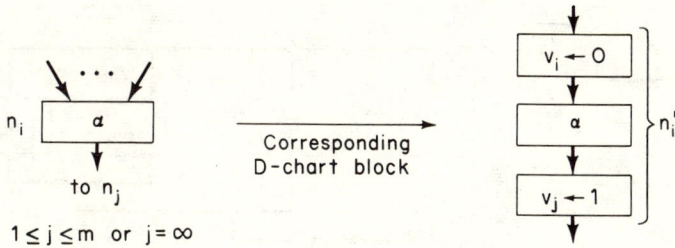

If n_i is a decision vertex, we construct a corresponding D-chart block as follows:

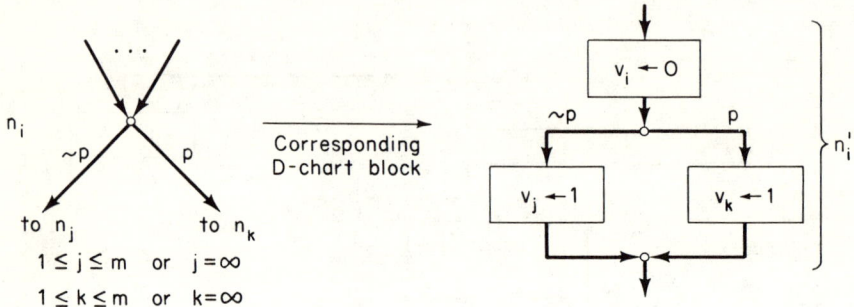

If N is the set of variables of F, we assume that $v_1,\ldots,v_m,v_\infty$ are not in N and that these new variables take on values in $\{0,1\}$. If n_i' is the D-chart block corresponding to vertex n_i in F we construct the following D-chart where we assume that n_j is the vertex in F which directly succeeds the START vertex ($1 \leq j \leq m$ or $j = \infty$) and $m \geq 1$ (if $m = 0$, then $D = \bar{F}$).

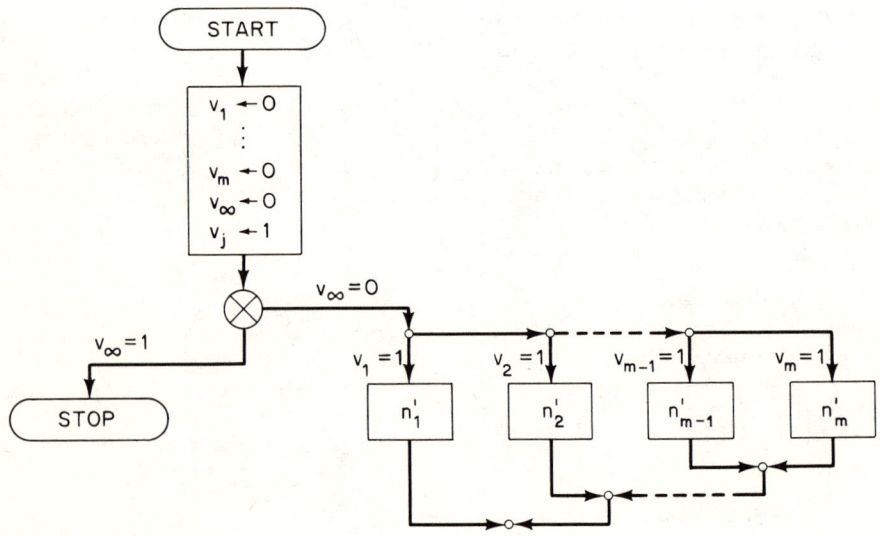

It is easy to see that $D\epsilon\xi(A)$.

Suppose $F\epsilon\xi_d(A)$ and R is the set of all atoms used in the formation of predicates associated with F. We say that a flow chart F' is *directly equivalent* to F *with respect to* A *and the atoms* R *of* F if $F'\epsilon\xi_d(A)$ and the predicates appearing in F' are formed using only atoms in R.

The following theorem is analogous to a theorem of Knuth and Floyd [2].

Theorem 2: There exists an algorithm A and a flow chart $F\epsilon\xi_d(A)$ such that there is no D-chart that is directly equivalent to F with respect to A and the atoms R of F.

Proof: Consider the following algorithm A and flow chart F, where $F\epsilon\xi_d(A)$:

$N = \{M,i\}$, $V_M = V_i = 1,2,\ldots$,
$S = \{s \mid s(M) \geq 1, s(i) = 1\}$, $C = \{c_1, c_2\}$, $R = \{p\}$
$c_1 \triangleq i \leftarrow 2M-i$
$c_2 \triangleq i \leftarrow 2M-2-i$
$p \triangleq i < M$

$$A(s) = \begin{cases} (c_2 c_1)^k & ; \ s(M) \text{ odd and } k = \dfrac{s(M)-1}{2} \\ c_2(c_1 c_2)^h & ; \ s(M) \text{ even and } h = \dfrac{s(M)-2}{2} \end{cases}$$

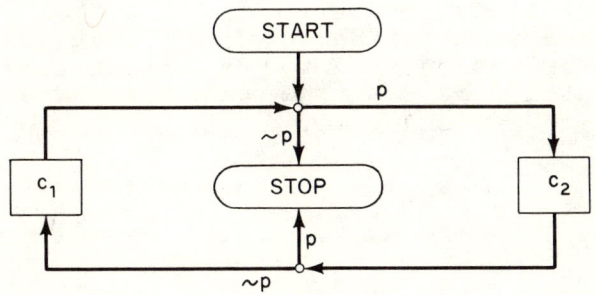

M	Sequence of values of i
1	$(\sim p)\, 1\, (\sim p)$
2	$(p)\, 1\ (p)\, 1\, (p)$
3	$(p)\, 1\ (p)\, 3\, (\sim p)\, 3\, (\sim p)$
4	$(p)\, 1\ (p)\, 5\, (\sim p)\, 3\ (p)\, 3\, (p)$
5	$(p)\, 1\ (p)\, 7\, (\sim p)\, 3\ (p)\, 5\, (\sim p)\, 5\, (\sim p)$
6	$(p)\, 1\ (p)\, 9\, (\sim p)\, 3\ (p)\, 7\, (\sim p)\, 5\, (p)\, 5\, (p)$
7	$(p)\, 1\ (p)\, 11\, (\sim p)\, 3\, (p)\, 9\, (\sim p)\, 5\, (p)\, 7\, (\sim p)\, 7\, (\sim p)$

The predicates in parentheses hold at their respective points in the sequence. Consider the following sequence of commands and predicates

$$\alpha = (p)\, c_2\, (\sim p)\, c_1\, (p)\, c_2\, (\sim p)\, c_1\, (p)\, c_2\, (\sim p)\, c_1\, (p)\, c_2\, (\sim p) \ldots$$

We interpret the above sequence as a meta-description of the execution of F for arbitrarily large M. Specifically, the subsequence of commands is the algorithm A(s) for arbitrarily large s(M); the predicate following each command holds after the corresponding command is executed, that is, (p) following c_1 means that i < M after c_1 is executed, and $(\sim p)$ following c_2 means that i $\geq$ M after c_2 is executed.

We make the assumption that there is a D-chart D that is directly equivalent to F, and we shall show that this leads to a contradiction. Let us "follow" the execution of D(s) when s(M) is arbitrarily large and suppose I is the first vertex in D that we visit for a second time. By the structure of D, I is an iteration vertex. The symbol (q) represents the atom (either p or $\sim p$) that was true when this loop was entered for the first time and (r) is the atom that was true when the vertex I was reached for the second time.

Expression of Algorithms by Charts 111

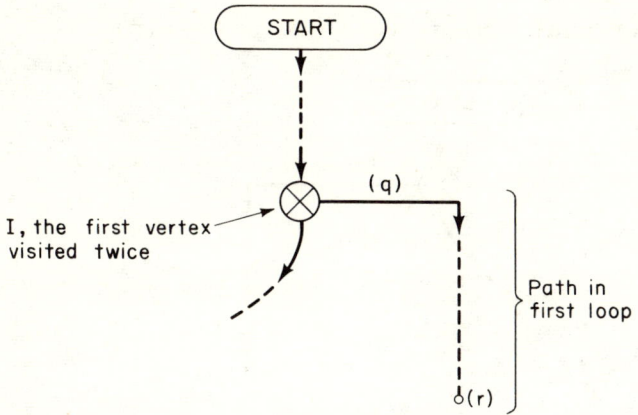

Assume that (q) = (p) and (r) = (~p). By inspection of α it is clear that

must appear on the path

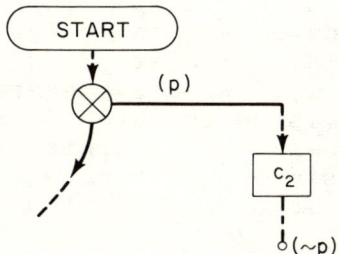

One can choose s'(M) such that D(s') behaves exactly like D(s) until

is reached for the first time, at which time in the execution of D(s'), c_2 causes p to be true and this is in fact the last command executed for this value of s'(M). This results in infinite looping and consequently (q) = (p) and (r) = (~p) cannot hold. A similar argument shows that (q) = (~p) and (r) = (p) cannot hold.

Assume that $(q) = (p)$ and $(r) = (p)$.

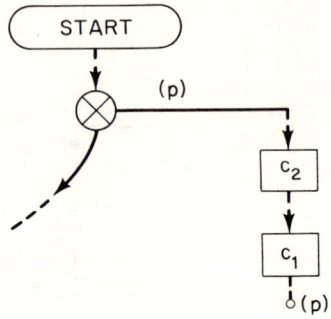

In this case

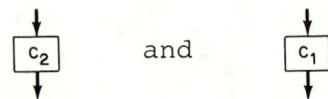

must appear at least one time as consecutive command vertices in the loop. Again by choosing $s'(M)$ properly we can cause p to hold after c_2 is executed for the first time in this loop. This again implies infinite looping, and consequently $(g) = (p)$ and $(r) = (p)$ cannot hold. Similarly, $(g) = (\sim p)$ and $(r) = (\sim p)$ cannot hold. We are therefore forced to conclude that there is no repeated vertex in the execution of $D(s)$ when $s(M)$ is arbitrarily large. This is impossible since D is finite and we can conclude that there is no D-chart that is directly equivalent to F.

FLAGS

In the proof of Theorem 1 we introduced the variables v_i in order to construct the appropriate D-chart, as did Bohm and Jacopini [3]. We can think of these variables as "flags" or "signlas" that tell us which sequence of commands to execute next. We can make the notion of a "flag" more precise. Let N be the set of variables associated with a flow chart F. We say that a variable $x \in N$ is a flag if x takes on values in a finite set, and in each command of the form $x \leftarrow f(y_1...y_m)$, each of the variables $y_1,...y_m$ are flags. The variable FOUND in the D-Chart that expressed algorithm SEARCH in Example 2 is a flag.

Intuitively one would think that flags are unessential in a flow chart, and in fact it is easy to show that they are dispensible in a certain sense For example, suppose we wanted to eliminate the flag FOUND in Example 2. Since FOUND takes on only two values, we can make two copies of D (considered as a flow chart), one with the value of FOUND considered to be "NO" and the other with FOUND set to the value "YES." Any statement that changes the value of FOUND is replaced by an appropriate transfer.

The following diagram shows two copies of D, one for each of the possible values of FOUND. The dotted edges are edges which have been omitted. A single START vertex has been added, and it is immediately followed by a test to determine the appropriate copy of D to begin with. The Figure 1 diagram can be reduced to a flow chart by successively eliminating all vertices with no incoming edges, replacing all series edges by single edges, replacing all parallel edges by single edges, and finally coalescing all the STOP vertices into a single STOP vertex. Applied to Figure 1, this procedure results in the flow chart F in Example 2.

We say that a set W of flags is complete if $x \leftarrow f(y_1,...,y_k) \varepsilon$ C and $x \varepsilon W$ imply $y_1,...,y_k \varepsilon W$. From the above example it should be clear that

Theorem 3: Let $F \varepsilon \xi_d(A)$ and W be a complete set of flags of F. For each $s \varepsilon S$ let $B(s)$ be the subsequence of $A(s)$ obtained by dropping all commands of the form $x \leftarrow f(y_1,...,y_k)$, where $x \varepsilon W$. Then there is a flow chart F' which one can construct from F such that $F' \varepsilon \xi_d(B)$.

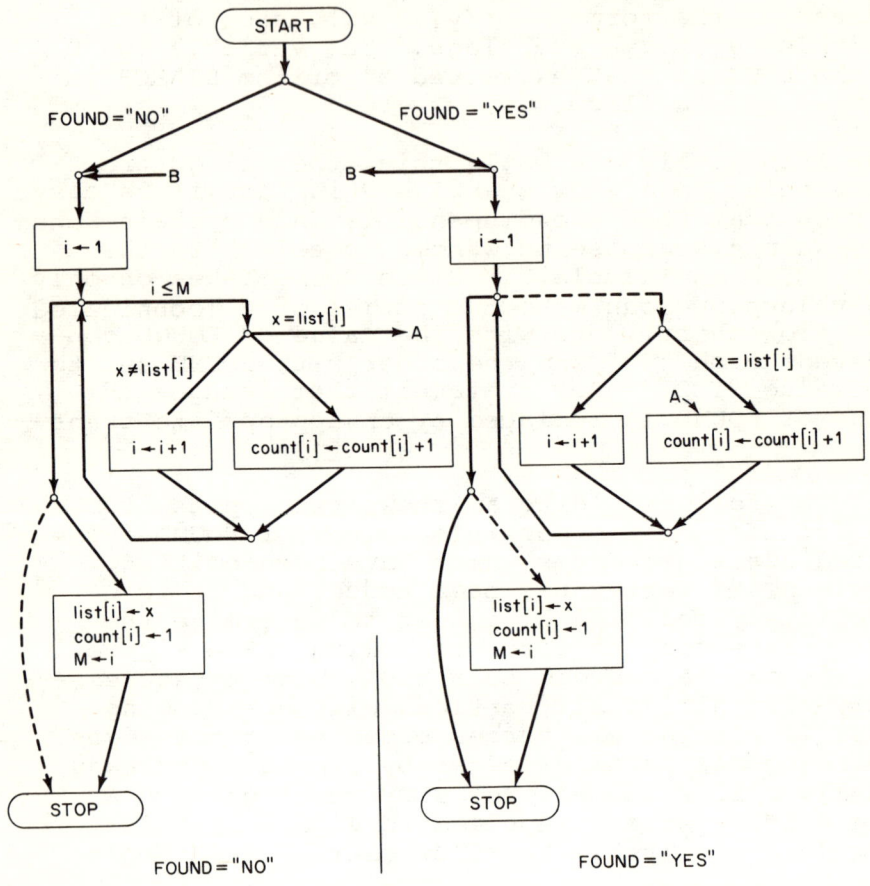

Figure 1

SUMMARY

The theorems of the previous sections are examples of results that might be misleading when applied to the problem of making an algorithm easy to understand. Theorem 1 means that D-charts are as powerful as flow charts if we are allowed to add flags to a given flow chart. However, the form of the D-chart given in the proof of the theorem is clearly not a desirable expression of an algorithm. The additional flags in the D-chart merely represent the topology of the original flow chart and this encoding of all the topology into flags does not necessarily make understanding the algorithm easy.

Theorem 3, on the other hand, shows that flags are superfluous since their effect can always be accounted for in the topology of a flow chart. This extreme is equally undesirable since a complex topology must be unraveled before an algorithm can be understood.

Finally, Theorem 2 indicates that we must necessarily permit the use of flags in D-charts if they are to be as powerful as arbitrary flow charts. This does not mean, however, that D-charts are an inadequate means of expression.

ACKNOWLEDGMENTS

This work was supported by the National Science Foundation under Grants GK-5535 and GJ-965, and by U.S. Army Research Office-Durham under Contract DAHC04-69-C-0012.

REFERENCES

[1] Dijkstra, E., "GoTo Statement Considered Harmful," *CACM*, 11:3, 1968, 147-148.

[2] Knuth, D.E., and R.W. Floyd, "Notes on Avoiding 'GoTo' Statements," *TR-CS 148*, Computer Science Department, Stanford University, 1970.

[3] Bohm, C., and G. Jacopini, "Flow Diagrams, Turing Machines and Languages with Only Two Formation Rules," *CACM*, 9:5, 1966, 366-371. 366-371.

AN INTERACTIVE SYSTEM FOR PROGRAM VERIFICATION

T. Lyons
John Bruno
Princeton University

This paper reports on an interactive programming system that allows verification of properties of a program. The GOTO-less language used to express algorithms is based on D-charts and is restricted to the data types integer and "node." Semantic statements (statements about the algorithm) are made in the first-order predicate calculus, and verification is achieved using "verification conditions" and mechanical theorem proving techniques such as "resolution." The use of a GOTO-less programming language greatly eases the problem of assigning semantic statements (predicates) and enables the exhibition of the dependence of "strongest verifiable conditions" on the entrance assertion and inductive hypothesis of every "while" clause.

INTRODUCTION

The logical validation of programs, based on the concepts advanced in Robert Floyd's paper "Assigning Meanings to Programs" [1], has attracted increasing attention. James King, for example, has demonstrated [2] that an interpretation-oriented theorem prover can establish the validity of a number of elementary algorithms in integer arithmetic. For the purpose of studying the problems peculiar to programs that primarily manipulate data structures and the formal proof techniques that are especially applicable to the validation process, we have designed an interactive system called VERIFIER.

In its present form VERIFIER accepts programs written in a skeletal structured language based on D-charts [3] and annotated with sentences of the first-order predicate calculus. Through a liberal definition of the semantics that may be assigned to a program statement, VERIFIER accommodates the segmentation of the tasks of constructing and validating a program. Rules of inference have been discovered that allow annotation using recursively defined predicate symbols that exhibit changes of state. The manual direction of mechanical refutation techniques has indicated what tasks VERIFIER must yet subsume autonomously before the process of verification becomes a convenient means of debugging programs.

ALGORITHM SPECIFICATION

The expression of algorithms in VERIFIER is done in a GOTO-less programming language. Flow of control is accomplished by using "*if-then-else*," "*while-do*," and "*begin-end*" constructions. Well-known algorithms, based on the introduction of Boolean flags, suffice to embed an arbitrary iterative program into a GOTO-less program. This transformation is possibly purchased at the price of merciless obfuscation. We advocate writing in the above style initially because it demands a mental discipline that facilitates annotation and verification.

D-charts provide a graphical representation for GOTO-less programs, which we shall use for expressing algorithms. The correspondence between syntax

and D-chart elements is displayed in Figure 1.
D-Charts of programs can be obtained from VERIFIER.

In all respects we have sought to retain a simplicity in syntax consistent with the provision of material with which to experiment. All identifiers are globally declared and a macro-definition facility (with no passing of parameters) is available. The two data types are integer and "node."

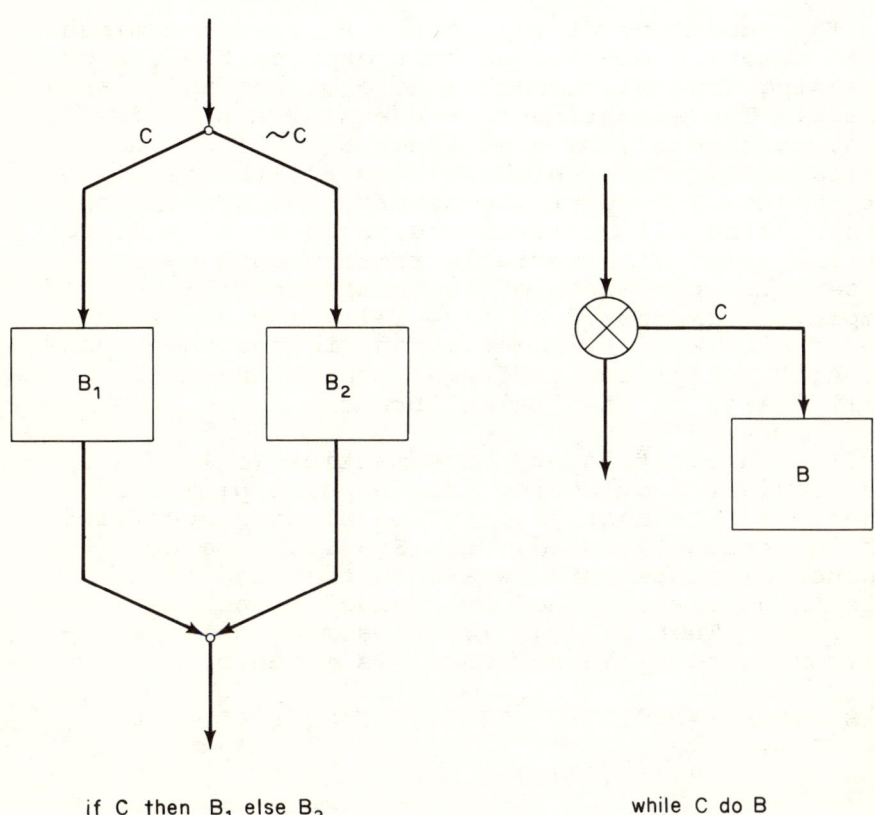

if C then B₁ else B₂   while C do B

Figure 1

The Correspondence Between GOTO-less
Syntax and D-Chart Elements

Identifiers can denote integer or pointer variables, fields, or multi-dimensional arrays. The minimal arithmetic operations are defined. Nodes comprise an intrinsically unconstrained set wherein links find their domain and range. Within this framework, however, even such constructions as recursive procedure calls can be imitated.

PROGRAM SEMANTICS

The semantics of a program, P, are determined by the semantic predicates that express the effect of passing control through a node of the associated D-chart. The semantics of traversing a path is given, in general, by a sentence $S(\xi,\xi')$ of the predicate calculus, which relates ξ', the final state vector. However, we observe the convention of supressing all declarations, such as x' = x, so that the value of a variable remains unchanged. The semantic predicate of the statement i ← i+1, for example, is expressed as i' = i+1. The decision node *if* A(i) > A(j), *then*... contributes the semantics A(i) > A(j) to its "true" branch and $\sim$ A(i) > A(j) to its "false" branch.

The calculation of the semantics (called a *path predicate*) of moving from a point p_1 in the D-chart of P to another point p_2 along a specified path is straightforward. Let $S_1 S_2 ... S_n$ be a sequence of statements, where in the case of a decision node the "true" or "false" branch is specified. Then $S_{12}(\xi,\xi')$, the semantics of passing from S_1 to S_n in sequence, is given by

(1) $S_{12}(\xi,\xi') = \exists \xi^1 ... \exists \xi^{n-1} S_1(\xi,\xi^1) \land S_2(\xi^1,\xi^2) \land ... \land S_n(\xi^{n-1},\xi')$

where $S_i(\cdot,\cdot)$ is the semantic predicate for statement S_i for i = 1,...,n.

A path predicate $S(\xi,\xi')$ may incorporate temporaries, in the form of existentially bound

Interactive System for Program Verification 121

variables, which cannot be removed during the process of forward substitution. For example, we prefer to defer expanding the description of an array to which multiple assignments have been made by introducing new symbols for its intermediate states. Further, the semantics that we shall allow to be assigned to the invocation of a macro will frequently be complex formulas.

PROGRAM ANNOTATION

The annotation of P consists of attaching to the the edges of its D-chart (or equivalently at points in the text of P) assertions $A(\xi)$, which purport to characterize the state vector at the particular point of the program. The verification of properties of P is attempted in terms of the assertions and semantics associated with P. For example, if $A_1(\xi)$ is an assertion at point p_1 of P, $S_{12}(\xi,\xi')$ is a path predicate from p_1 to p_2, and $A_2(\xi)$ is an assertion at point p_2, then the validity of

(1) $\quad A_1(\xi) \wedge S_{12}(\xi,\xi') \rightarrow A_2(\xi')$

implies that if $A(\xi)$ is true at p_1 and then the execution of P follows the path associated with $S_{12}(\xi,\xi')$, then $A_2(\xi')$ will be true at p_2.

A program may be said to be sufficiently annotated when it has been endowed with an *input assertion* $A_0(\xi)$ and *inductive assertions* $A_i(\xi)$, for $i = 1,\ldots,m$, numerous enough to interdict all the loops of the program. Under these circumstances there are but a finite number of (simple) paths along which control can flow from one assertion to another — hence a finite number of formulas of the form

(3) $\quad\quad\quad A_i(\xi) \wedge S_{ij}(\xi,\xi') \rightarrow A_j(\xi')\quad\quad$.

Suppose that each of the formulas (3) is valid and that the input assertion $A_0(\xi)$ is true for an input state ξ_0. It follows at any future time during the execution of P that if ξ' is the current state at the point p_j to which the jth inductive assertion is attached, then $A_j(\xi')$ must be true.

More generally, consider an arbitrary point p, and let

$$S_{ip}^{(k)}(\xi,\xi')$$

range over the semantic predicates associated with simple paths from an inductive assertion or input condition to p. Then one of the following sentences is true of the current state ξ' at p

(4) $$\exists \xi (A_i(\xi) \wedge S_{ip}^{(k)}(\xi,\xi'))$$

— namely, the one associated with the path along which control most recently flowed to p.

THE VALIDATION TASK

Owing to the limitations placed on branching in GOTO-less programs, one obtains a sufficiently annotated program by attaching inductive assertions to the "true" branch of each "while" clause. Henceforth, we assume P to be endowed with precisely this set of *inductive assertions*. Let $A_i(\xi)$ adorn the ith while clause for $i = 1,\ldots,m$, and for a point p in P, let C_{ip} denote the collection of simple control paths from the right branch of the ith while clause to p. If $\gamma \in C_{ip}$, then let $S_\gamma(\xi,\xi')$ be the associated path predicate. Given the annotation, the strongest possible consequence that can be derived at the point p is

(5) $$\bigvee_{\substack{i=0,\ldots m \\ \gamma \in C_{ip}}} \exists \xi_0 (A_i(\xi_0) \wedge S_\gamma(\xi_0,\xi)).$$

An assertion $B(\xi)$ at p can be inferred from the annotation if it is not stronger than this strongest possible consequence, or equivalently if

(6)
$$\bigvee_{\substack{i=0,\ldots m \\ \gamma \varepsilon C_{ip}}} \{A_i(\xi) \wedge S_\gamma(\xi,\xi') \to B(\xi')\}$$

is valid.

The *output assertion* $B(\xi)$ at the exit point p of the program should, in particular, satisfy formula (6). This requirement along with the validity of the formulas (3), may be incorporated into the following statement: *The problem of proving a program correct consists of verifying that the annotation by inductive assertions is consistent and potent, that is, that each inductive assertion and the output assertion follows from the strongest possible consequence at its respective location.*

As it stands, of course, the validation of formula (6). This requirement, along with the validity of formulas (3), may be incorporated of the formula

$$\bigvee C_i \to \bigwedge D_j$$

is equivalent to the concurrent validity of the formulas $C_i \to D_j$, one casts the consistency of an annotation as the problem of proving that the individual conjuncts of an inductive assertion are implied by the strongest possible consequence obtained along each of the several control paths that flow from another inductive assertion or the initial condition. To have a machine merely handle the bookkeeping required to propagate forward the semantic path predicates and define the theorems that must be proved is a great convenience.

THE SEMANTICS OF MACRO-STATEMENTS

The construction of an algorithm of moderate complexity can often be facilitated by generating it from the top down, in the manner proposed by Dijkstra [4] and recently demonstrated by Hoare [5], proceeding to a more detailed specification of its components only after they have been properly coordinated at a higher level of abstraction. The accommodation of this style of programming in a system for verification requires the ability, first, to define the meaning of higher level operations and, second, to confirm this meaning in more detailed specifications. In practice, VERIFIER permits the unconstrained assignment of semantic predicates $S(\xi,\xi')$ to the macro statements with a program and expects the annotator to justify his assignments through validation of the macro-text. The foregoing of this incidental validation is equivalent to extending the basic language. New symbolic statements, posed as dummy macros, may be defined by their effect on the environment.

But to ensure that the semantics delcared during the top-down generation of an algorithm are, indeed, realizable requires the validation of macros. Let a macro-text be prefixed by the copying of its initial program state ξ into a static vector ξ_0; in fact, only those components need be copied to which comparison will be made upon exit and that will be rewritten before exit. Annotation of the text may then be made in terms of the new state vector (ξ_0,ξ), as in the example of Figure 2. *If $P(\xi)$ is the input assertion and $Q(\xi_0,\xi)$ is the output assertion of the validated text, then semantics as strong as $P(\xi) \rightarrow Q(\xi,\xi')$ may be attached to its invocations. Conversely, $S(\xi,\xi')$ constitutes a valid semantic predicate, if it can be inferred as a valid output assertion from the input assertion "true."*

The judicious replacement of complicated D-chart segments by appropriately semanticized macros mitigates the validation task, because the number of formulas, (3), to be established is the number

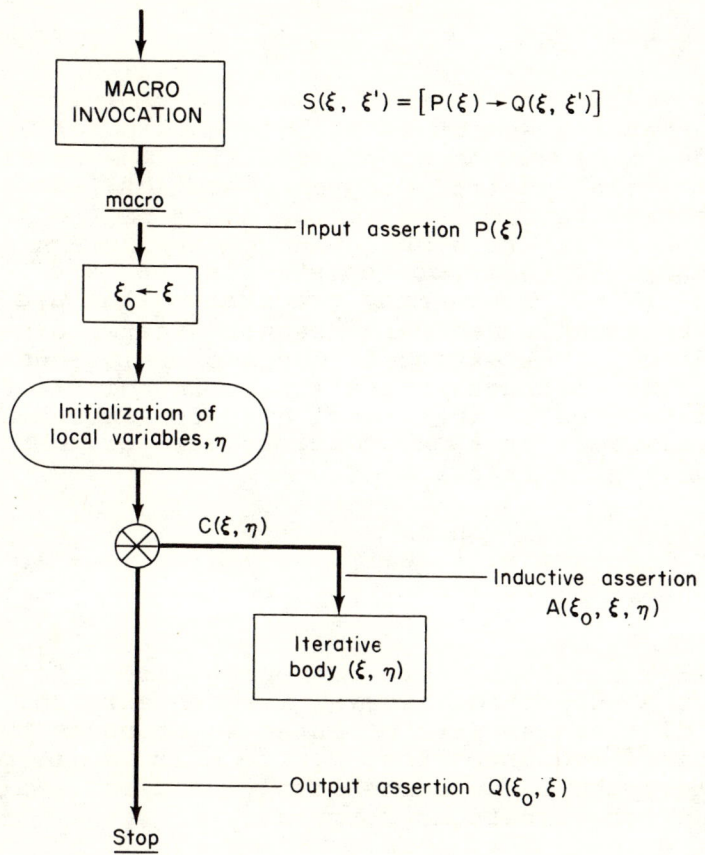

Figure 2

The Replacement of an Iterative Routine by a Macro Invocation. Semantics No Stronger Than Those Indicated May be Attached to the Invocation.

of simple paths between inductive assertions. Isolating a deeply nested iterative routine from the major inductive assertions removes an annoying source of control paths.

PREDICATE SYMBOLS

The discussion to this point has tacitly assumed that the semantics $S(\xi,\xi')$ and inductive assertions $A(\xi)$ can be compounded from the primitive predicates that control program execution. In fact, we observe the need to introduce to the annotation predicate symbols whose meaning *cannot* be expressed in terms of the symbols that are known to the program. Many predicates that are characteristically recursive cannot otherwise be accommodated. The extended successor relations in a complex data structure are a case in point. Symbolic predicates are useful also for subsuming functionals such as the summation operator. Writing sigma(sum,m,n,a) in place of

$$\text{sum} = \sum_{i=m}^{n} a(i)$$

is equally useful and more convenient; both notations require the support of several inference rules. One can distinguish sets of integers or nodes by introducing predicates that denote membership, or predicate symbols can quite simply be used as a shorthand for cumbersome formulas.

Each predicate symbol that is introduced must be accompanied by a set of inference rules that delimit its *meaning*. Sometimes the rules will define templates or schema that can be considered universally valid, available to the theorem prover as axioms at all points of the program, e.g., rules for inequalities. At other times the predicates will be recursively defined in terms of variable and function symbols belonging to the program. Then the predicate symbol itself exhibits changes of state that must be recorded during the process of forward substitution.

As the terms that enter into the description of a recursively defined predicate are rewritten, the predicate itself undergoes a possibly violent change. Consider, for example, a recursive predicate symbol D defined by the formula $\text{Defn}(\xi,D)$. Suppose $A_1(\xi,D)$ and $A_2(\xi,D)$ are assertions at points p_1 and p_2 in P, respectively, and that $S_{12}(\xi,\xi')$ is the path predicate associated with a simple path from p_1 to p_2, then the validity of

(7) $\quad A_1(\xi,D) \wedge S_{12}(\xi,\xi') \rightarrow A_2(\xi',D')$

implies that if $A_1(\xi,D)$ is true at p_1 and execution of P follows the path associated with $S_{12}(\xi,\xi')$, then $A_2(\xi',D')$ will be true at p_2. The axioms $\text{Defn}(\xi,D)$ and $\text{Defn}(\xi',D')$ can, of course, be used in a refutation. The important feature to notice about (7) is that there is no term that directly relates D' to D, and, moreover, the change in D cannot, in general, be mechanically deduced. Indeed, the inference rules that describe the predicate do not, in general, secure it unambiguously.

Our remedy for this difficulty is to insist on a description of these recursive predicate symbols in terms of their previous states, which means in terms of equation (7) that one must include in the path predicate terms that relate D' and D. In the general case, let Ψ be the vector of recursive predicate symbols used in annotating P, the semantics of traversing a path is given by a sentence $S(\xi,\xi',\Psi,\Psi')$ in the predicate calculus and the general form for equation (1) is

(8) $\quad S_{12}(\xi,\xi',\Psi,\Psi') = \exists \xi^1 \ldots \exists \xi^{n-1} S_1(\xi,\xi^1,\Psi,\Psi^1) \wedge$
$\quad \quad S_2(\xi^1,\xi^2,\Psi^1,\Psi^2) \wedge \ldots \wedge S_n(\xi^{n-1},\xi',\Psi^{n-1},\Psi')$

Verification of the *asserted* changes, to the extent that it is possible, will be done by the theorem prover as a separate problem.

The transitive closure of a relation appears to us to be a sufficiently useful and prevalent construction as warrants some ability to manipulate it mechanically. Accordingly, we interpret the equation $D(x,y) = *A(x,y)$ as meaning that D is the least predicate that satisfies

(9) $\quad D(x,y) \longleftrightarrow x = y \vee A(x,y) \vee \exists z[D(x,z) \wedge D(z,y)]$.

Elementary inferences such as equations (10) and (11) follow from the definition of D. Beyond this, resolution of two conflicting transitive closures proceeds on the basis of rules such as (12) and its reflection:

(10) $\quad [A(x,y) \to A'(x,y)] \to [D(x,y) \to D'(x,y)]$

(11) $\quad D(x,y) \wedge x \neq y \to A(x,y) \vee \exists z] z \neq x \wedge A(x,z) \wedge D(z,y)]$

(12) $\quad D(x,y) \wedge \sim D'(x,y) \to \exists z_1 \exists z_2 [D(x,z_1) \wedge A(z_1,z_2) \wedge D(z_2,y) \wedge D'(x,z_1) \wedge \sim A'(z_1,z_2)]$.

The validation of programs that have been annotated with the limits of theorem proving in mind can be supported by just such inference rules. Indeed, these rules prove adequate to deduce the perturbation to D which results from such an expansion of A as occurs during the course of elementary algorithms.

 One explanation for the difficulties frequently encountered in drawing deductions from formulas which involve recursive predicate symbols is that those predicates which exhibit changes of state embody a great deal of information which is not being recorded in program variables and functions. One does, in fact, encounter instances in which augmenting the program by an explicit temporal

variable and a vector of periodic snapshots allows
the substitution of explicit comparisons with past
states, grounded on elementary literals, for a more
intractable recursive predicate. One cannot hope,
however, to replace conveniently the extended
successor relations in complex data structures,
which are instances of the transitive closure. The
need to manipulate diverse predicate symbols,
externally imposed upon a program, requires techniques of formal theorem proving beyond whatever
interpretation-oriented mechanisms may have been
adapted to the programming language itself.

EXAMPLE: TREESORT

An example of an annotated program that illustrates many of the points made above, albeit
gratuitously, is the treesort algorithm of Figure 3.
A binary tree is grown by successively inserting the
elements of an array $a(1), \ldots, a(n)$ into the tree
in such a manner that the left subtree of any node
contains only lesser values than the node itself
and the right subtree only greater values. Following
a Fortran-like naming convention to distinguish
pointer from integer types, we use p, q and r to
denote pointer variables and $t\ell$, tr to denote the
left and right-link fields of the binary tree. We
constantly denote the root of the tree by r, and ϕ
denotes a distinguished node that will mimic a
null link.

The main routine of treesort iterates the macro
INSERT. INSERT strikes a path into the tree from
the root, looking for the proper place to deposit
a_0. The semantics of INSERT are involved, first,
because they reflect two alternative outcomes —
namely, the discovery that a_0 is already in the tree
or that it is necessary to create a new node to
accommodate it — and, second, because the second
outcome demands a description of how the data
structure has changed. INSERT itself calls on the
macro GETQ to allocate a node that is not already
in the tree. The existence of such a node can be

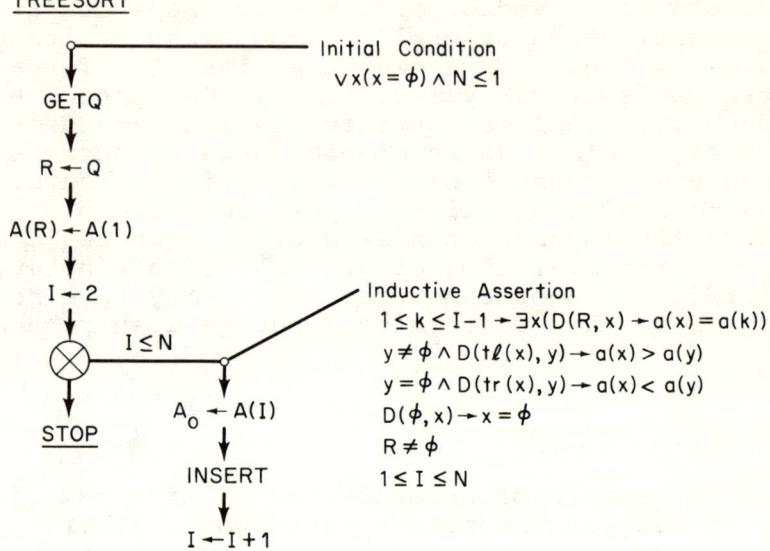

INSERT Semantics

$\exists z(D(R,z) \land a(z) = a_0 \land D' = D \land a' = a \land t\ell' = t\ell \land tr' = tr) \lor$

$\exists z(\sim D(R,z) \land D'(R,z) \land [D'(z,x) \to x = z]$

$\land\, a'(z) = a_0 \land (x \neq z \to a'(x) = a(x))$

$\land\, [t\ell'(x) = t\ell(x) \lor t\ell'(x) = z] \land t\ell'(z) = \phi$

$\land\, [tr'(x) = tr(x) \lor tr'(x) = z] \land tr'(z) = \phi$

$\land\, [D(x,y) \to D'(x,y)] \land [D'(x,y) \to D(x,y) \lor y = z]$

$\land\, [D'(t\ell'(x), z) \to a'(x) > a_0] \land [D'(tr'(x), z) \to a'(x) < a_0])$

GETQ Semantics

$\sim D(R, Q') \land Q' \neq \phi \land t\ell(Q') = \phi \land tr(Q') = \phi$

Figure 3

An Annotation of the Treesort Algorithm

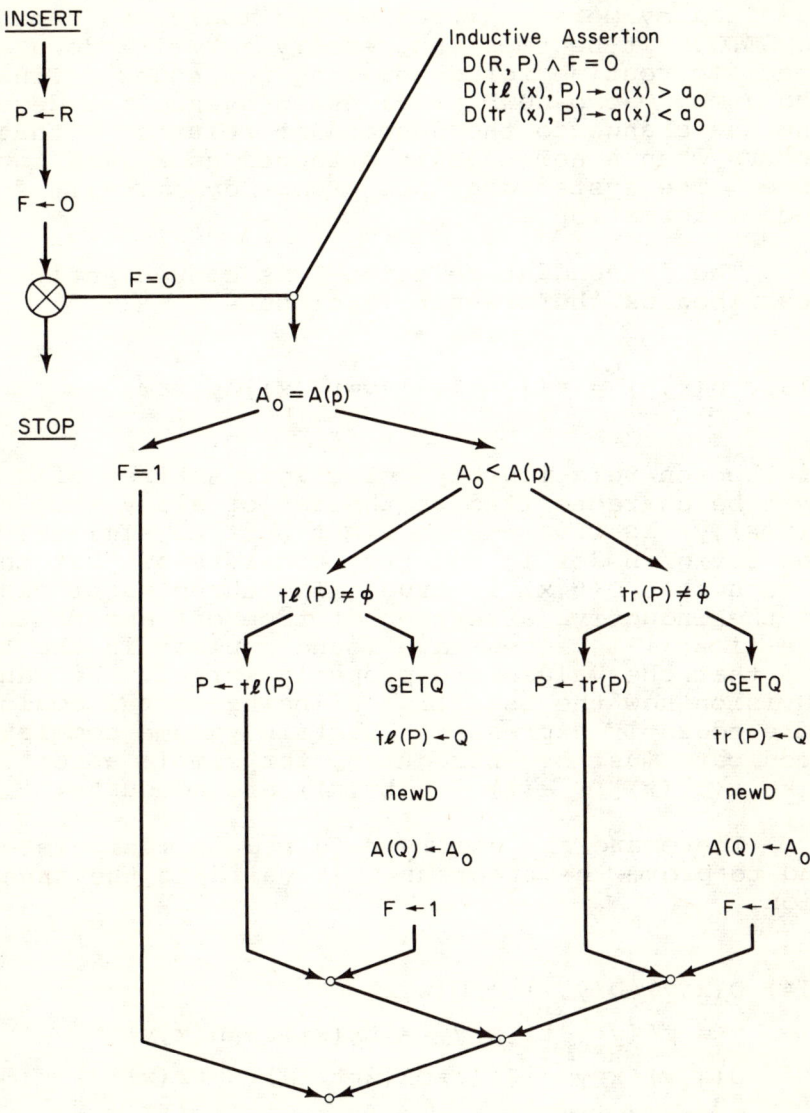

"newD" declares: $D'(x,y) \leftrightarrow D(x,y) \vee [y = Q \wedge D(x,P)]$

Figure 3 (continued)

asserted by merely attaching the indicated semantics to GETQ. It becomes unnecessary to write down a specific routine for generating new nodes. Finally, the dummy macro newD provides an avenue for describing the change to the descendant relation D that occurs when a new node is attached as a leaf to the tree. The system does not prompt dynamically for such information.

The descendant relation D is conveniently described as the transitive closure

(13) $\quad D(x,y) = *([y=t\ell(x) \vee y=tr(x)] \wedge y \neq \emptyset)$

of the son relationship. The left subtree of x can then be characterized as the set of all y such that $D(t(x),y)$ is true — the right subtree similarly. The set of nodes in the tree consists of just those x such that $D(r,x)$ is true. The three major clauses of the inductive assertion of treesort assert that the first i-1 values have found a place in the tree and that the values are properly sorted. We cannot envision how the assertion of being sorted could be more cogently expressed. Certainly some complex predicate must be introduced, for simple assertions like $a(t\ell(x)) < a(x) < a(tr(x))$ are adequate.

There are six axioms required to manipulate D and to prove the theorems that validate the annotation:

(14) $\quad D(x,y) \wedge D(y,z) \rightarrow D(x,z)$

$\quad\quad y \neq \emptyset \wedge (y = t\ell(x) \vee y = tr(x)) \rightarrow D(x,y)$

$\quad\quad D(x,y) \wedge x \neq y \rightarrow \exists z (z \neq \emptyset \wedge (z=t\ell(x) \vee z=tr(x)))$

$\quad\quad D(x,t\ell(y)) \rightarrow x = t\ell(y) \vee D(x,y)$

$\quad\quad D(x,tr(y)) \rightarrow x = tr(y) \vee D(x,y)$

$\quad\quad \sim D(t\ell(x),r) \wedge \sim D(tr(x),r)$

The first three are consequences of D's definition.

Interactive System for Program Verification   133

The last three require the special knowledge that D describes descent in a tree. Given the description of a tree below, one can derive these further axioms and can validate the annotation at newD on the basis of such inferences from the transitive closure as were described above.

Specifically, one postulates in the special case of a tree that

(15) $tr(x) = t\ell(y) \to tr(x) = \emptyset \land t\ell(y) = \emptyset$

$x \neq y \land t\ell(x) = t\ell(y) \to t\ell(x) = \emptyset \land t\ell(y) = \emptyset$

$x \neq y \land tr(x) = tr(y) \to tr(x) = \emptyset \land tr(y) = \emptyset$

$D(t\ell(x),x) \lor D(tr(x),x) \to x = \emptyset$

$x \neq \emptyset \longleftrightarrow D(r,x)$

$t\ell(\emptyset) = \emptyset \land tr(\emptyset) = \emptyset$

Should one insist on a more thorough validation of treesort, it becomes necessary to assert the formulas of (15) inductively and to strengthen the semantics of INSERT. The semantics of GETQ must also be expanded into a more explicit allocation scheme; the semantics as they stand contradict the fifth clause. The complexity of the annotation thus increases to the point where the essential mechanism of the algorithm is obscured. The validation task also grows to encompass, in effect, the establishment as lemmas of what were listed in (14) as reasonable axioms. For an algorithm as easily comprehended as treesort it would be folly to pursue the annotation beyond what we have given.

The more complex programs that we aspire to validate will be granted access to a library of formulas, which characterize such data structures as binary tree, list, and queue, and a library of transformations that render them invariant. For example, tree(d,r,tℓ,tr) might serve as an abbreviation for the formulas

(16) $D(x,y) = *[(y = tl(x) \lor y = tr(x)) \land y \neq \emptyset]$
$D(r,x) \land D(r,y) \land tr(x) = tl(y) \rightarrow tr(x) = \emptyset \land tl(y) = \emptyset$
$D(r,x) \land D(r,y) \land x \neq y \; tl(x) = tl(y) \rightarrow tl(x)$
$\qquad\qquad\qquad\qquad\qquad\qquad = \emptyset \land tl(y) = \emptyset$
$D(r,x) \land D(r,y) \land x \neq y \; tr(x) = tr(y) \rightarrow tr(x)$
$\qquad\qquad\qquad\qquad\qquad\qquad = \emptyset \land tr(y) = \emptyset$
$D(r,x) \rightarrow \sim D(tl(x),x) \land \sim D(tr(x),x)$
$r \neq \emptyset$

It then need be verified only once that tree(D',r, tl',tr) is the consequence of tree(d,r,tl,tr) and the following semantic transformation:

(17) $D(r,p)$ $\qquad\qquad tl(p) = \emptyset$
$D(x,q) \lor D(q,x) \rightarrow x = q \qquad q \neq \emptyset$
$tl'(p) = q \qquad\qquad x \neq p \quad tl'(x) = tl(x)$
$D'(x,y) \longleftrightarrow D(x,y) \lor (y = q \land D(x,p))$

These semantics can be assigned to a macro named "insert q as the left leaf of p."

Note that as one admits to consideration nodes external to the tree being observed, one must explicitly restrict quantifications to the range $\{x:D(r,x)\}$. Sets of nodes can somewhat more easily be distinguished by explicitly maintaining their characteristic functions as additional fields in every node. Nonetheless, the complexity of the theorems that must be proved creates an awesome task for one who attempts to manage data structures on the elementary level of assigning links.

To return to our example, however, it might be of interest to witness a deduction that is a small part of the validation of treesort. We choose to show that

(18) $y \neq \emptyset \land D(t\ell(x),y) \rightarrow a(x) > a(y)$

remains true throughout an iteration of the primary loop. We shall assume that a node has been added to the tree during INSERT; that is, we shall consider only the following alternative of the path predicate:

(19) $a_0' = a(i) \quad i' = i+1$
$D(r,z_0) \quad D'(r,z_0) \quad D'(z_0,x) \rightarrow x = z_0$
$a'(z_0) = a_0' \quad x \neq z_0 \rightarrow a'(x) = a(x)$
$t\ell'(x) = t\ell(x) \lor t\ell'(x) = z_0$
$tr'(x) = tr(x) \lor tr'(x) = z_0$
$t\ell'(z_0) = \emptyset \quad tr'(z_0) = \emptyset$
$D(x,y) \rightarrow D'(x,y)$
$D'(x,y) \rightarrow D(x,y) \lor y = z_0$
$D'(t\ell'(x),z_0) \rightarrow a'(x) > a_0'$
$D'(tr(x),z_0) \rightarrow a'(x) < a_0'$

We wish to show that these formulas imply

(20) $y \neq \emptyset \land D'(t\ell'(x),y) \rightarrow a'(x) > a'(y)$

We proceed via refutation, as a machine would, but we do not attempt to mimic any machine-level strategy. The detailed argument appears in the Appendix. Hopefully, it is clear from the context that x and y denote free variables and that z_0, x_0, y_0 denote constants generated through the introduction of Skolem functions.

This argument is typical of what we have seen so far in that it proceeds most easily through the mechanisms of positioning in turn the alternatives of a distinguished disjunction, of instantiating free variables to derive a ground clause, and of inferring from two ground clauses a third. Direction is provided by the heuristic of seeking to eliminate primed symbols. We have discovered that resolution directed entirely by a person at the console is infeasible because of a frequent multiplication and recombination of literals, upon passing to conjunctive normal form, that obscures the import of a supposedly unsatisfiable formula. Where resolution can easily be steered to the goal of a refutation, one finds that it is so because a preference for unit ground clauses provides sufficient guidance.

THE SCOPE OF MECHANICAL ASSISTANCE

The present design of VERIFIER accommodates a number of modules that permit refutations from conjunctive normal form to be derived manually. The assistance that they provide is primarily in the field of bookkeeping; they prevent the oversight of details that confounds pencil and paper simulations of mechanical procedures. Resolution, instantiation, substitution, the manipulation of inequalities, and the positing of the alternative disjuncts of a clause are techniques that appear adequate to the task of validating annotations from which the perturbations of recursive predicates can be excised or deferred. Sophisticated resolution strategies and unification in its general form seem to be required only for the automatic verification of the state changes of predicates. Otherwise path predicates embody enough specific terms and ground clauses to provide a refutation. Indeed, if no inductive assertion or macro-semantic is existentially quantified, then set-of-support theorems demonstrate that the validation of a consistent annotation can be based on resolution with pairs of clauses at least one of which is a ground clause. In any case, simplifications can be made upon such systems, such as that of Allen and Luckham [6] merely because the reconstruction of proofs has no interest for us.

Our current interest is in the attempt to exploit interaction to a greater degree by allowing the computer to generate all the resolvents of whatever ground clauses lie in the theorem-proving buffer, in coordination with useful instantiations of other clauses selected by the annotator. In the event that a refutation is not discovered, the response of the machine will be to offer up a small number of the more concise new consequences that it may have discovered. The selection of alternative disjuncts and the preference for eliminating certain terms through substitution will be determined by the annotator. Failing a refutation, the response of the machine can be expected to indicate either that more detailed guidance will approach a refutation or that the current annotation requires greater strengthening and precision. This aid will be all the more appreciated to the extent that the response can be prefaced by a deconversion from conjunctive normal form to the parlance of human logic.

One of the problems that confronts us is the inherent complexity of descriptions of data structures from the primitive level of nodes and link fields. The verification of real programs would seem to suggest the desirability of investigating the problems of annotating in such detail, which is what encouraged us to choose the elementary programming language that we did. Better methods for defining predicates over a set of nodes, whose structures are constantly changing, are sorely needed. Many compromises were made in our annotation of treesort to cut down to reasonable size the allocation routine GETQ and the axiomatization of the descendant relation D. Currently it is merely a hope that by operating with recursive predicates on a macroscopic level and by defining acceptable semantics for common transformation of data structures, and other large-scale operations, we can establish properties of programs that are more complex than the sorting algorithms that have thus far received attention.

ACKNOWLEDGMENTS

This work was partially supported by the National Science Foundation under Grant GK-5535.

REFERENCES

[1] Floyd, R.W., "Assigning Meanings to Programs," *Proc. Symposia in Applied Mathematics*, Vol. 19, American Mathematical Society, 1967, 19-32.

[2] King, J., "A Program Verifier," Ph.D. thesis, Carnegie-Mellon University, 1969.

[3] Bruno, J., and K. Steiglitz, "The Expression of Algorithms by Charts," This volume.

[4] Dijkstra, E.W., "Structured Programming," [EWD 249], T.H.E. (privately circulated).

[5] Hoare, C.A.R., "Proof of a Program; FIND," *CACM*, 14:1, January 1971, 39-25.

[6] Allen, J.R., and D. Luckham, "An Interactive Theorem-Proving Program," *Machine Intelligence 5*, Edinburgh University Press, 1970, 321-336.

APPENDIX: AN EXAMPLE OF A REFUTATION FROM TREESORT

1. $y_0 \neq \emptyset$ denial of conclusion
2. $D'(t\ell'(x_0), y_0)$ denial of conclusion
3. $a'(x_0) \leq a'(y_0)$ denial of conclusion
4. $t\ell'(x) = t\ell(x) \vee t\ell'(x) = z_0$ path predicate
5. $t\ell'(x_0) = t\ell(x_0) \vee t\ell'(x_0) = z_0$ 4
6. <u>assume</u> $t\ell'(x_0) = z_0$
7. $D'(z_0, y_0)$ 2,6
8. $D'(z_0, x) \rightarrow x = z_0$ path predicate
9. $y_0 = z_0$ 7,8
10. $D'(t\ell'(x_0), z_0)$ 2,9
11. $D'(t\ell'(x), z_0) \rightarrow a'(x) > a_0$,   path predicate
12. $a'(x_0) > a_0$,   10,11
13. $a'(z_0) = a_0$,   path predicate
14. $a'(y_0) = a_0$,   9,13
15. $a'(x_0) \leq a_0$,   3,14
16. <u>contradiction</u>   12,15

6. <u>otherwise</u> $t\ell'(x_0) \neq z_0$
7. $t\ell'(x_0) = t\ell(x_0)$ 5,6
8. $D'(t\ell(x_0), y_0)$ 2,7
9. $D'(x,y) \rightarrow D(x,y) \vee y = z_0$ path predicate
10. $D'(t\ell(x_0), y_0) \rightarrow D(t\ell(x_0), y_0) \vee y_0 = z_0$ 9

11. $D(t\ell(x_0), y_0) \lor y_0 = z_0$ 8,10
12. <u>assume</u> $y_0 = z_0$
13. $D'(t\ell'(x_0), z_0)$ 2,12
14. $D'(t\ell'(x), z_0) \to a'(x) > a_0$,   path predicate
15. $a'(x_0) > a_0$,   13,14
16. $a'(z_0) = a_0$,   path predicate
17. $a'(y_0) = a_0$,   12,16
18. $a'(x_0) \leq a_0$,   3,17
19. <u>contradiction</u>   15,18

12. <u>otherwise</u> $y_0 \neq z_0$
13. $D(t\ell(x_0), y_0)$ 11,12
14. $D(t\ell(x), y) \to a(x) > a(y)$ inductive assertion
15. $a(x_0) > a(y_0)$ 13,14
16. $x = z_0 \lor a'(x) = a(x)$ path predicate
17. $y_0 = z_0 \lor a'(y_0) = a(y_0)$ 16
18. $a'(y_0) = a(y_0)$ 12,17
19. $x_0 = z_0 \lor a'(x_0) = a(x_0)$ 16
20. <u>assume</u> $x_0 = z_0$
21. $t\ell'(z_0) = \emptyset$ path predicate
22. $t\ell'(x_0) = \emptyset$ 20,21
23. $t\ell(x_0) = \emptyset$ 7,22
24. $D(\emptyset, y_0)$ 13,23

25.	$D(\emptyset,x) \to x=\emptyset$	inductive assertion
26.	$y_0 = \emptyset$	24,25
27.	<u>contradiction</u>	

20.	<u>otherwise</u> $x_0 \neq z_0$	
21.	$a'(x_0) = a(x_0)$	19,20
22.	$a(x_0) \leq a(y_0)$	3,18,21
23	<u>contradiction</u>	15,22